THE
MEDIEVAL
WORLD

Philip Steele

KING*f*ISHER

CONTENTS

KINGFISHER

Kingfisher Publications Plc
New Penderel House, 283–288 High Holborn,
London WC1V 7HZ
www.kingfisherpub.com

Material in this edition previously published by Kingfisher
Publications Plc in the *Best-Ever* series

This edition published by Kingfisher Publications Plc 2006
10 9 8 7 6 5 4 3 2 1

1TR/0106/TWP/(FR)150SEM

Copyright © Kingfisher Publications Plc 1995, 1998, 2006

A CIP catalogue record for this book is available from
the British Library.

ISBN-13 978 0 7534 1373 9
ISBN-10 0 7534 1373 6

Printed in Singapore

The first knights

Soldiers had fought on horseback throughout the early Middle Ages, but it was only after the 9th century that mounted troops became seen as a special or élite force. They were now the key to their lord's struggles for power.

▼ At dawn, over 900 years ago, Norman ships are run on to a shelving beach. Men wade through the waves with supplies and lead kicking and whinnying horses ashore. The knights' forces might be attacked at any time, so they quickly check their weapons and their long, kite-shaped shields.

The Normans were descended from Vikings, fierce Scandinavian warriors who had been granted a large area of northern France in 911. Normans went on to seize many other parts of Europe, invading England in 1066 and Sicily in 1072. Their knights were tough, adventurous and often brutal.

Stirrups

Mounted warriors became a deadly force because of the stirrup, a Chinese invention which reached Europe in the 8th century. These supported the rider's legs, steadying him so that he could strike with greater force.

▲ The Bayeux Tapestry is a long embroidered panel showing scenes from the Norman invasion of England in 1066. The Norman Duke William conquered the country and became king. He rewarded his loyal knights by giving them large areas of land, so many of them settled in England.

THE AGE OF CHIVALRY

Imagine travelling back to Europe in the Middle Ages. Two great armies are facing each other. A warrior covered in shining armour grips his sword, as his warhorse stamps the ground. Suddenly a shout goes up and the knights begin their charge... The word 'knight' originally meant 'servant', but in most languages the word for 'knight' meant 'horseman'. Knights were in fact soldiers who swore loyalty to their lord or king. As servants, they were far from lowly. Over the years knights became powerful and highly respected.

stirrup

5

The medieval world

Medieval society was very different from our own. At the top of every country was a duke, prince, king or emperor. People believed that he alone had a God-given right to rule. The ruler gave land and privileges to the great lords of the country, if they promised to support him and fight for him when necessary. A knight would promise to fight for one of these lords in return for his protection and some land.

▲ A person who held land from another was called a vassal. He had to swear loyalty to his lord. The social system depended on oaths of allegiance.

Here, Jean de Sainte-Marie swears loyalty to King René of France.

► A knight looks on as fresh horses are brought from the castle to his party. Other travellers on the road have joined his family to take advantage of his protection. These include a priest and a monk as well as a pilgrim and a lawyer.

A life of toil

Poor people called serfs had few rights. They had to work the land and were not allowed to leave their village. Their crops fed the lord in his castle, as well as their own families, and in turn the lord was meant to protect them.

▶ Strong fortresses were needed to protect a knight's land and the people who worked it. After the 1100s stone walls increasingly replaced wooden ones. These were reminders of the power of kings, lords and knights.

◀ Poor people spent all their lives working to produce food. But in 1348, many people in Europe died of a terrible plague called the Black Death. Fewer workers meant that they could bargain for wages.

▲ The poor had no opportunities and just tried to survive. But as the Middle Ages continued some people improved their lives through education or by learning a trade. These people, who included lawyers and merchants, could afford to travel on business, or even go on a pilgrimage, the nearest thing the Middle Ages got to a holiday.

If a king ruled unfairly, a powerful lord could claim the throne. In turn a knight was under no obligation to a lord who broke faith with him.

This social organization, the 'feudal system', began to break down during the Middle Ages. It had been based on land, but money was becoming more important. Kings needed money to fight wars. They borrowed it from bankers, who soon became richer than kings.

Crisis in Christendom

Duringthe Middle Ages, Europe was made up of many small kingdoms, principalities and duchies, all jostling for power. English kings ruled large areas of France. German emperors spent as much time in their Italian lands as at home. The Byzantine empire stretched from what is now west Turkey into Greece.

▲ In 1095 Pope Urban II preached to crowds at Clermont in France. He called for knights all over Christendom to launch a holy war, or Crusade, against the Saracens.

▼ Moslem Arabs had conquered all of north Africa by 705. The first Moslem attack on Spain in 711 was followed by two further waves of Moorish invasion, in 1087 and again in 1147. They built fine palaces there, and cities such as Córdoba became centres of scholarship where Moslems, Jews and Christians lived side-by-side in peace. It took over 700 years for Christian knights to reconquer all of Spain.

▶ During the 12th century the Normans who had invaded England in 1066 seized new lands in Wales, Scotland and Ireland. Royal marriages and conquest extended the English rule over large areas of France.

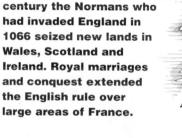

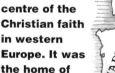

SCOTLAND

IRELAND

ENGLAND

WALES

DANES

LONDON

CANTERBURY

HAMBURG

BRITTANY

NORMANDY

PARIS

WORMS

COLOGNE

MAINZ

HOLY ROMAN EMP.

GERMANY

AUGSBURG

MILAN

CLERMONT

BURGUNDY

GENOA

BORDEAUX

TOULOUSE

CORSICA

FLOREN

COMPOSTELA

LEON

NAVARRE

ARAGON

BARCELONA

SARDINIA

ROM

CASTILE

PORTUGAL

TOLEDO

VALENCIA

CORDOBA

SEVILLE

GRANADA

ALMORAVIDS

MEDITERRANEAN SEA

▶ Rome was the centre of the Christian faith in western Europe. It was the home of the pope, who was thought to be God's representative on Earth.

Medieval Europe

In 1100 many of today's countries had not yet been formed. People were often loyal to their feudal lord rather than to a nation.

All these lands were held together by the Christian faith, and so were known as Christendom. Christendom was bordered by peoples of other faiths. Moslem Arabs and Berbers, known as Moors, ruled a large area of Spain as well as north Africa. Their fellow Moslems to the east were known to the Christians as Saracens, and included Arabs, Turks and Kurds. Fierce warriors from central Asia, known as Tartars or Mongols, attacked eastern Europe.

NOVGOROD

RUS

KIEV

By 1206 a central Asian ruler known as Genghis Khan had united all the Mongolian tribes. Their warriors soon rode west to devastate Russia, Poland and Hungary.

POLAND

PRAGUE

HUNGARY

BELGRADE

▼ The city of Jerusalem and the lands around it were holy to Christians, Moslems and Jews. From 1096 onwards this Holy Land was the scene of the Crusades, a series of bloody wars in which Christian knights fought the Saracens for control.

BLACK SEA

CONSTANTINOPLE

BYZANTINE EMPIRE

MEDITERRANEAN SEA

ITALY

APULIA

ITALIA

RUM (ICONIUM)

▶ Travel was difficult during the Middle Ages. The fine roads of the Roman empire fell into ruin. Horses and wagons had to struggle on muddy or dusty tracks. At sea, small ships were at the mercy of storms and pirates.

RHODES

CRETE

CYPRUS

ANTIOCH

BAGHDAD

SELJUK EMPIRE

TRIPOLI

DAMASCUS

ACRE

JERUSALEM

ARAB   NOMADS

ALEXANDRIA   FATIMID CALIPHATE

CAIRO

Chivalry

The ideals of chivalry were celebrated in public with splendid ceremonies, colourful banners and fanfares of trumpets. Dress became more and more elaborate – and impractical to wear. Strict rules governed every detail of a knight's behaviour, whether fighting, hunting, dressing or dining.

▼ Knights and their retainers ride through the streets of a French town. They have been summoned to their lord's court for a wedding celebration. A noblewoman gazes down at the passing group. She is looking forward to the banquets and festivities in the castle. She may be able to arrange a wealthy match for her daughter, or find a courtly champion to further her own interests.

For big occasions such as a knighting ceremony or a tournament, vassal knights gathered from throughout the lord's lands, and confirmed their homage and loyalty to him. This was a chance to discuss news from abroad and the local countryside, the stores of food and arms, plans for battles or defence.

The knight's code

The first knights were simply soldiers on horseback, but from the 12th century on they were expected to follow a strict code of honour. Inspired by Christian teachings, knights were meant to have courteous and gentle manners. They saw themselves as part of a noble, superior class of people. The word 'chivalry' (from 'cheval', the French word for horse) came to stand for these ideals. Chivalry did inspire knights, but rarely prevented brutality or treachery.

Courtly love

This shield was made in Flanders in about 1475, for parading at a mock battle or tournament. It shows a knight swearing loyalty to a lady. Women had few rights in the early Middle Ages, but chivalry demanded that noble ladies were honoured and protected. This 'courtly love' had little to do with real love or marriage. It was a romantic ideal dreamed up by poets in Brittany, southern France and Moorish Spain.

◄ Children's play was good practice for fighting.

▼ A boy's first horse might be made of wood and have wheels, and his first lance might be a broom handle.

The page

It was best to start learning all the skills of knighthood at an early age. Young boys of seven or so were often sent to another castle as a page, waiting at table and learning good manners.

Becoming a knight

To become a knight you had to be a man, even if women did sometimes go on Crusades. You were supposed to come from an aristocratic family, although some people lied about their history. You needed money or land, for being a knight was expensive. An ambitious young man would try to marry into a noble family in order to gain wealth and status. Finally, you had to prove yourself in battle.

spur

sword

▲ The growing page learned how to ride properly. He then learned to charge at a quintain, a wooden target that was sometimes designed to swing round and knock him down if he was slow and clumsy.

As a sign of becoming a knight, another knight would tap you on both shoulders with a sword (or cuff you on the side of the head, in the early days). To celebrate Whitsun in 1306, King Edward I of England held a Feast of the Swans at Westminster. The king knighted his eldest son, who in turn knighted about 300 other young noblemen.

The Maid of Orléans

Although women could not become knights, in 1429 a simple country girl did join the French in besieged Orléans and then lead the attack on Paris, dressed in armour. Joan of Arc had heard the saints' voices, telling her to save France from the English. She inspired the French knights but was later captured and burnt as a witch.

▼ **In the yard of the castle, a soldier taught the young lads to fight, using wooden or blunted weapons. They could also keep fit by wrestling and swimming.**

The squire

At about 14 years old, the page became a squire. His job was to help a knight prepare for battle and to fight at his side.

The knight

After about four years of experiencing warfare, the squire could become a new knight, and be 'dubbed'. Often the squire would undergo a vigil, a night of prayer, before the ceremony. Swords and gilt spurs were symbols of knighthood that the new knight could now wear.

◄ A Teutonic Knight stands watch over the Order's lands on the River Vistula. In the 13th century the Teutonic Order, veterans of the Crusades, joined with the Knights of the Sword of Livonia to fight in central and eastern Europe.

Knightly orders

Knights who were fighting holy wars sometimes formed special groups. These were based on the orders of monks, and their members took religious vows. The three most famous orders grew up during the Crusades in the Holy Land. The Knights of St John were founded in 1099. The Knights Templar were founded in 1119. The Teutonic Order was founded by German knights in about 1190.

▼ The French king Philip the Fair wanted the riches of the Knights Templar for himself. He accused them of witchcraft and black magic, and from 1307 to 1314 he had them arrested, tortured and killed. In 1314 the leader of the Templars, Jacques de Molay, was burned.

All three orders built castles and battled against the Saracens, becoming very powerful and wealthy. Many rulers feared the power of these knightly orders. So they decided to found their own orders of chivalry, such as the Garter in England, the Annunciata in Savoy and the Golden Fleece in Burgundy. Membership of these orders conveyed honour to the knights.

◀ **The Knights Templar were a fighting order from the start, but prayer still played a part in their daily routine. They were based in a wing of the royal palace in Jerusalem, thought to be the site of the temple of Solomon – hence their name. The knights were mostly French, but they also had branches in Spain and the British Isles.**

▼ **Sweating under his helmet, a Knight of St John charges out against the Saracens. The Knights of St John began as a religious order, praying and caring for wounded knights and Christian pilgrims. They were often referred to as 'Hospitallers', after their hospital in Jerusalem.**

▼ **Though the main orders of knighthood began in the Holy Land, later they looked for other homes and their influence spread throughout Europe. Spain also had many orders dedicated to fighting the Moors from north Africa.**

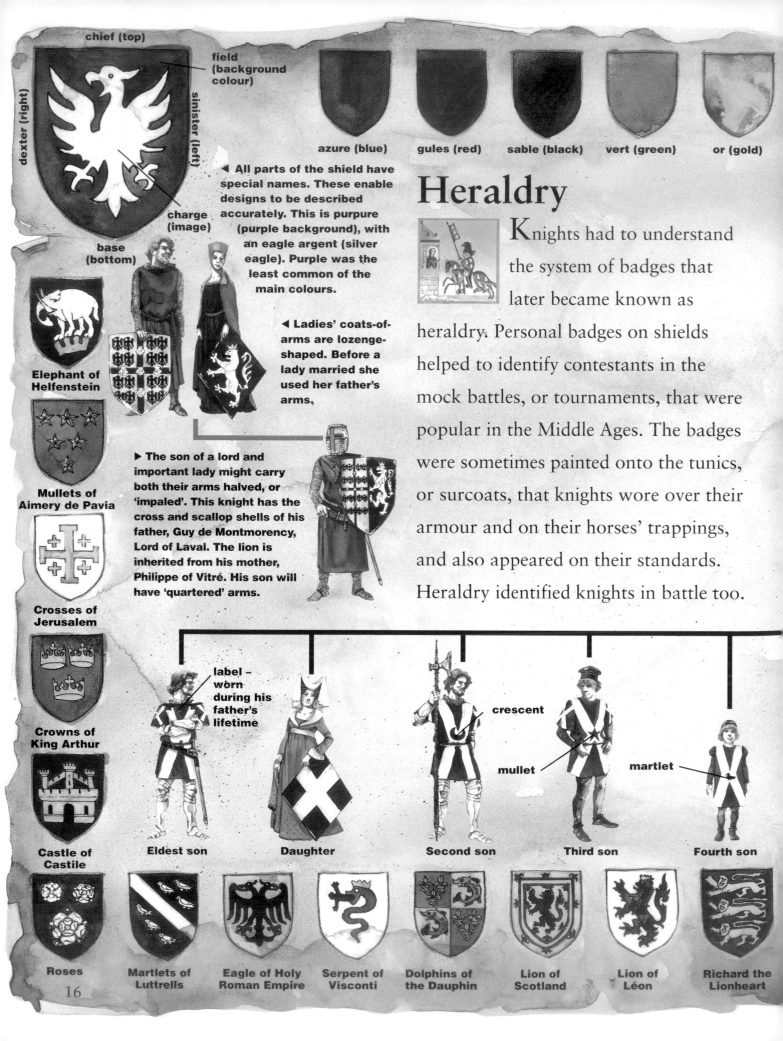

chief (top)

field (background colour)

dexter (right)

sinister (left)

charge (image)

base (bottom)

azure (blue) gules (red) sable (black) vert (green) or (gold)

◀ All parts of the shield have special names. These enable designs to be described accurately. This is purpure (purple background), with an eagle argent (silver eagle). Purple was the least common of the main colours.

◀ Ladies' coats-of-arms are lozenge-shaped. Before a lady married she used her father's arms,

▶ The son of a lord and important lady might carry both their arms halved, or 'impaled'. This knight has the cross and scallop shells of his father, Guy de Montmorency, Lord of Laval. The lion is inherited from his mother, Philippe of Vitré. His son will have 'quartered' arms.

Heraldry

Knights had to understand the system of badges that later became known as heraldry. Personal badges on shields helped to identify contestants in the mock battles, or tournaments, that were popular in the Middle Ages. The badges were sometimes painted onto the tunics, or surcoats, that knights wore over their armour and on their horses' trappings, and also appeared on their standards. Heraldry identified knights in battle too.

Elephant of Helfenstein

Mullets of Aimery de Pavia

Crosses of Jerusalem

Crowns of King Arthur

Castle of Castile

label – worn during his father's lifetime

crescent

mullet

martlet

Eldest son

Daughter

Second son

Third son

Fourth son

Roses

Martlets of Luttrells

Eagle of Holy Roman Empire

Serpent of Visconti

Dolphins of the Dauphin

Lion of Scotland

Lion of Léon

Richard the Lionheart

ermine

vair

per pale

per fess

per bend

per chevron

per cross

per saltire

gyronny

checky

per fess engrailed

per pale nebully

per bend sinister indented

per bend embattled

Even today we still use the term 'coat-of-arms' to describe a heraldic shield badge. Coats-of-arms were passed down from father to eldest son. They became family badges, a sign of noble birth. They appeared on the seals of documents and today may still be seen in castle halls and on medieval tombs.

The rules of heraldry were laid out in great detail and each colour, pattern or other design had its own special description, or 'blazon', detailed in an old version of the French language.

▲ Five basic colours, or 'tinctures', were used in heraldry, with two 'metals' – gold and silver. There were also patterns based on furs, of which vair and ermine are two. A metal could only be placed on a tincture or vice versa. Blue and gold were popular in France, and black and gold in Germany. The 'field' could be divided by straight or jagged lines. Standard shield patterns were called 'ordinaries'. But others had all kinds of charges, or images, such as elephants and roses.

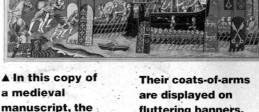

▲ In this copy of a medieval manuscript, the Knights of the Holy Ghost are shown boarding ship for the Crusades.

Their coats-of-arms are displayed on fluttering banners, shields and on the long pavises which protected them from enemy archers.

baton sinister – this mark shows that the son is illegitimate

Illegitimate son

◄ If a coat-of-arms was a badge for the whole family, then there still had to be a way of telling its various members apart. Within a family, different children or generations were identified by 'marks of difference'. The system varied from one country to another. These six people are all children of the English Earl of Westmoreland. Each has his or her own mark.

The herald

The herald was an official serving a king or great lord, who had to know a great deal about coats-of-arms. It was he who carried messages between the warring armies and identified dead knights.

canton

saltire

cross

pile

chevron

pale

fess

chief

FORTRESS HOMES

The great age of castles began almost 1,000 years ago and lasted for nearly 500 years. During this time, over 15,000 castles stretched across the lands of Europe and the Near East. They towered over the valleys of the River Rhine in Germany and the Seine in France. They guarded lonely mountain passes in Scotland and Wales, and they were battered and besieged in the scorching heat of Spain, Sicily and Syria.

Crusader castle
The castle of Krak des Chevaliers was originally an Arab fortress. It was taken over and rebuilt by Christian knights during the wars of the Crusades. These took place in the 1100s and 1200s when Christians fought against Muslims called Saracens.

▼ Krak was a military base which could hold over 2,000 men. Its powerful defences survived 12 sieges before it was finally captured in 1271.

▲ In times of peace, a castle's lord and lady held great feasts and wore their finest clothes.

Castles were built in an age of war. These powerful strongholds were used to control and defend large areas of the surrounding countryside. They were a base from which a lord and his soldiers could launch attacks on their enemies. With their high towers and thick walls, castles also provided protection against the fiercest of enemy assaults. But a castle was much more than a fortress. Inside its walls there might be a magnificent hall, comfortable chambers and a beautiful chapel. A castle was the home of its lord, his family and his followers – and they could live there in style.

Building a castle

It is the year 1290 and a great stone castle is being built. There are no power drills or bulldozers as there are on a modern building site. Most of the work is done by muscle power. Carpenters saw wood and assemble the scaffolding. Blacksmiths make and mend tools. Masons shape stone, and labourers curse and sweat as they haul heavy loads, mix up mortar for the walls and dig trenches.

Mason's marks

Every mason had his own special mark. He often carved this design into the stone he was working on, a bit like a painter signing his name on a painting. The marks were also used to work out how much each mason should be paid.

Raising the walls

Scaffolding was made of wood (1). It was slotted into openings in the stonework called putlog holes (2). For extra strength, a castle's main walls were packed with stone rubble and flints mixed with mortar (3). Walls could be between 2 and 5 metres thick.

Masons

A master mason was hired to design the castle and take charge of its building (4). Directly under him were freemasons who cut and carved the stone (5), and roughmasons who built the walls (6).

Lifting loads

Ropes and pulleys were used to lift buckets full of materials and beams (7). Heavy stones were raised by a treadwheel crane, turned by a man walking inside a giant wheel (8).

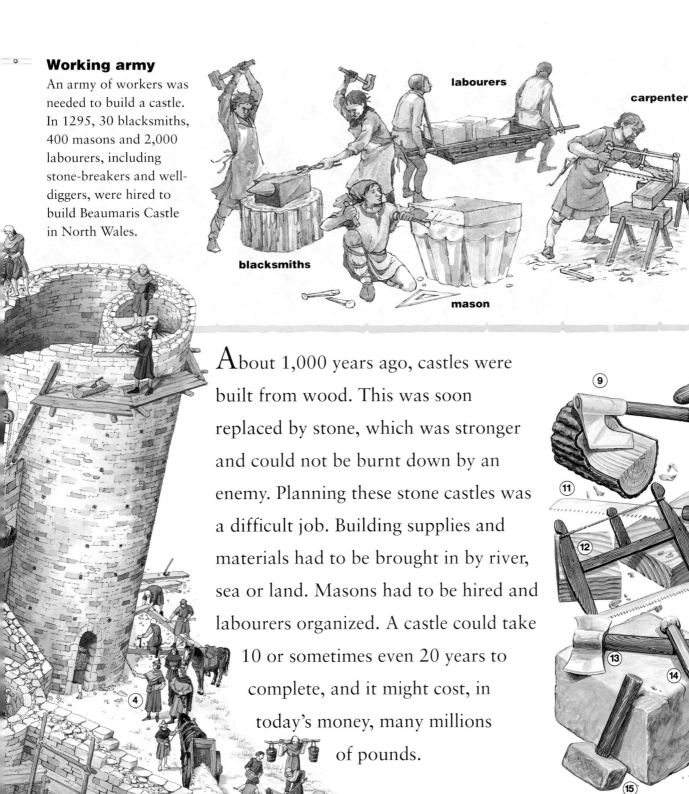

Working army

An army of workers was needed to build a castle. In 1295, 30 blacksmiths, 400 masons and 2,000 labourers, including stone-breakers and well-diggers, were hired to build Beaumaris Castle in North Wales.

labourers

carpenter

blacksmiths

mason

About 1,000 years ago, castles were built from wood. This was soon replaced by stone, which was stronger and could not be burnt down by an enemy. Planning these stone castles was a difficult job. Building supplies and materials had to be brought in by river, sea or land. Masons had to be hired and labourers organized. A castle could take 10 or sometimes even 20 years to complete, and it might cost, in today's money, many millions of pounds.

Tools of the trade

A carpenter used an axe (9), an awl (10), a saw (11) and a handsaw (12). A mason used a mason's axe (13), a chisel (14) and a mallet (15).

21

Clues to the past

Today, most castles lie empty or in ruins. Their defences are shattered, their walls bare, and their great halls silent except perhaps for the whistling wind. However, with a little detective work it's easy to find clues and work out what a castle looked like in the Middle Ages.

1 The keep

It's usually easy to find the keep – the largest building standing in the heart of the castle. Its outer walls would have once been whitened with lime to dazzle the eye.

2 Stone walls

In some castles, you may be able to see a trace of faded coloured plaster on the inside walls. The plaster was once painted with bold, bright patterns, or hung with richly woven tapestries.

3 The gatehouse

Grooves in the wall at the entrance show where the portcullis was raised and lowered. The portcullis slid down the grooves to make a gate. Behind were two heavy wooden doors.

So why did so many castles become ruins? By the end of the 1400s, wars were being fought in open country, not around castles, and kings and nobles no longer needed to live in fortified homes. Instead, they chose to live in more comfortable houses, and castles were left empty and deserted.

4 Fireplaces

High up in the walls are the remains of fireplaces. Look out for rows of small square holes beneath them. These once held joists – the timbers that supported the floors.

5 The chapel

Where was the castle chapel? Look out for rows of arched windows, finely carved stonework and a stone basin in one of the walls. The basin would have held water to rinse the cup used during religious services.

6 Wall defences

Can you see holes in the stonework of the outer walls? In times of war these supported the beams of wooden platforms called hourds.

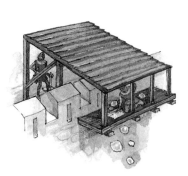

7 Spiral stairs

In the towers, see how the stone staircases wind up and round to the right. An enemy knight fighting his way up would hold his sword in his right hand and would have little space to use it properly.

8 The moat

Is there a dry, grassy ditch? Once, this would have been filled with water to keep the enemy at a distance.

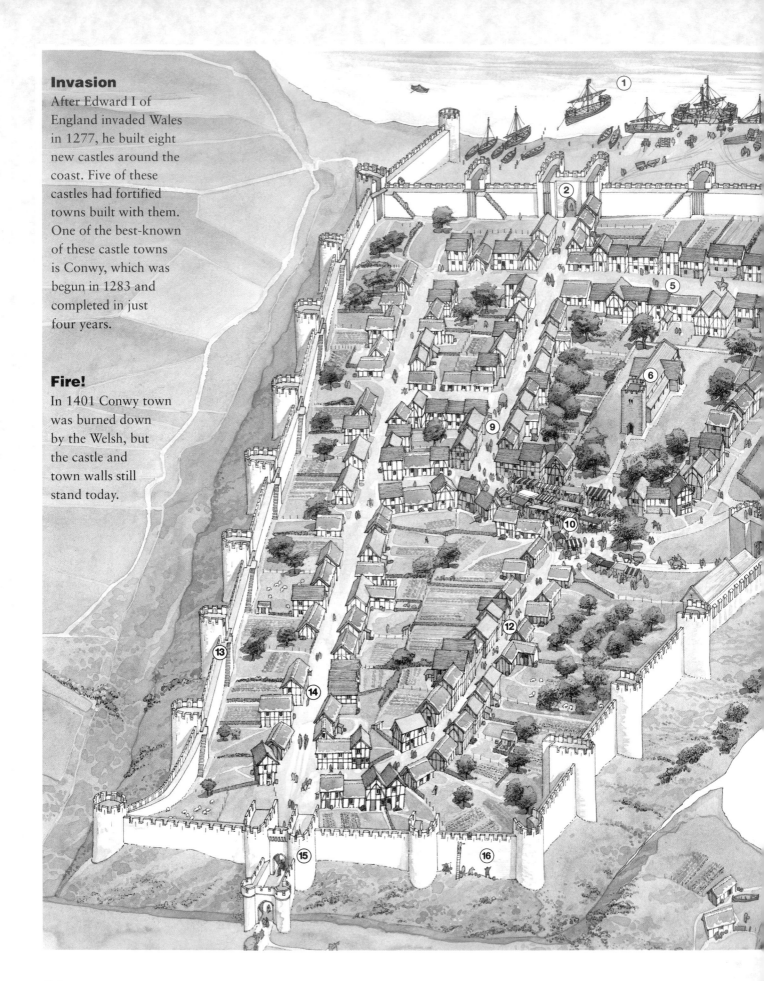

Invasion

After Edward I of England invaded Wales in 1277, he built eight new castles around the coast. Five of these castles had fortified towns built with them. One of the best-known of these castle towns is Conwy, which was begun in 1283 and completed in just four years.

Fire!

In 1401 Conwy town was burned down by the Welsh, but the castle and town walls still stand today.

The town of Conwy

1. harbour
2. lower gate
3. postern gate
4. Conwy Castle
5. Castle Street
6. St Mary's Church
7. Llywelyn's Hall
8. water mill
9. High Street
10. market square
11. mill gate
12. Rosemary Lane
13. wall walk running all the way around the town
14. Upper Gate Street
15. upper gate
16. gang of workers painting the town walls white

A castle town

Many towns in the Middle Ages were protected by a castle. Sometimes the castle was built long after the town had grown up. Sometimes the town grew up around an existing castle's walls. In newly-conquered lands, however, a castle and town were usually planned as one unit and their walls were put up at the same time. These new towns were often settled by people who were loyal to the castle's lord.

Master mason

Edward I hired the greatest castle-builder in Europe, Master James of St George from Savoy (now part of France). Master James was responsible for building all of Edward's castles in North Wales. He designed Conwy Castle so that its massive walls formed part of the town's own wall defences.

▲ Important towns had their own seal. Conwy's seal, pictured here, dates from about 1320.

Gates and walls

In times of trouble, the gatehouse of a castle town would have been well guarded, with soldiers on sentry duty day and night. The sentries were usually real busybodies, searching carts and baskets and asking strangers awkward questions. Traders on their way to market probably had to slip the guards a bribe – a jug of ale, a pie or perhaps a silver coin, and an unwelcome visitor could expect an arrow in the throat.

◀ **The coat of arms of the City of Lancaster, England.**

▲ **London was ringed by defensive walls and was protected by the Tower of London (the 'White Tower').**

Independence

Castle towns displayed the lord's badge or coat of arms above their gates. Some towns, however, had their own coat of arms to show that the townsfolk did not live under the shadow of a castle or lord. The townspeople paid the lord rent in return for their freedom. These towns were usually fortified, with high walls, gatehouses and even a small army.

A great city

In the early 1300s, London had about 80,000 people and was one of the largest towns in Europe. Other towns were usually smaller, with under 2,000 people.

Curfew hour

At night, a bell was rung and the doors of the town were shut and barred. No one could then enter or leave until daybreak. The bell was also the signal for the townsfolk to cover their fires with dome-shaped clay pots before going to bed. The pots were called curfews (from the French word *couvrefeu* meaning to cover fire).

▶ **As there wasn't enough land inside a town's walls for growing crops or keeping animals, the townsfolk had to buy food from local farmers.**

Town defences

In times of trouble, an enemy attacker would have to get through the town's defences before reaching the castle itself. As towns had exactly the same sort of defences as the castle, this was no easy task. Armed soldiers protected the town's long wall walks, and the gatehouses could be sealed off by heavy, timber-framed portcullises, studded with iron. The soldiers fired arrows through narrow slits called 'loops' built into the walls.

Town houses

Many town houses had wooden frames. The spaces between the timbers were filled with wattle and daub – criss-crossed sticks plastered with clay (1).

Market day

Most castle towns held a market once or twice a week. On market day, the town square would be filled with bustling crowds and traders shouting their wares. Visitors could buy anything from candles, shoes and knives to a refreshing draught of ale. A couple of times a year there was also a fair, which was bigger than a market and sold many more goods.

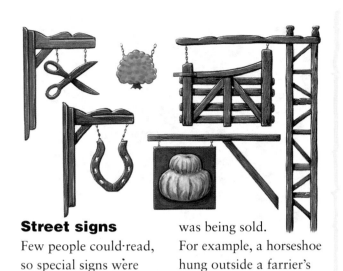

Street signs

Few people could read, so special signs were hung outside shops so that people knew what was being sold. For example, a horseshoe hung outside a farrier's and a green bush was the sign for an inn.

Muddy streets

Streets were very muddy and dirty as there were no proper drains, just open ditches where water and rubbish collected (2). They were also very smelly – waste was simply thrown out of the windows!

Goods for sale

Goods produced locally, such as pottery (3), purses and belts (4), were sold by the craftsmen who made them. Luxury items – finely woven cloth (5) or decorated jugs and bowls (6) from Italy – were brought to market by merchants.

Entertainers

Even if you couldn't afford the fine goods on sale, it only cost a farthing or a halfpenny to watch stilt-walkers and jugglers (7) or perhaps a dancing bear (8).

Learning a trade

Many young lads in the town became apprentices. They were sent to live with the family of a master craftsman and learned his skills. After seven years they were free to leave and set up on their own.

▶ **A cooper taught his apprentice the craft of barrel-making.**

In many towns, craftsmen and merchants belonged to societies called guilds. The guild controlled prices, organized training, and made sure that goods were of a high standard. Often, craftsmen's workshops were found in one street or area of a town. Some town streets still carry the name of the traders who worked there, such as 'Threadneedle Street' or 'Ironmongers Lane'.

Moneylenders

Nobles and even kings sometimes needed to borrow money, to pay craftsmen or fight wars. Some moneylenders, therefore, became very rich.

▶ **When coins became worn out, they were bought by weight.**

1 Hourds

Wooden hourds were fitted to the battlements. Gaps in the floor of the hourds allowed soldiers to drop missiles on to the heads of anyone below.

2 Battlements

The tops of the walls had solid parts called merlons which helped to shelter the defenders during an enemy attack. The defenders could fire through gaps called crenels which had wooden shutters for extra protection.

3 Drawbridge

The wooden drawbridge could swing up like a seesaw so that no one could cross the ditch.

30

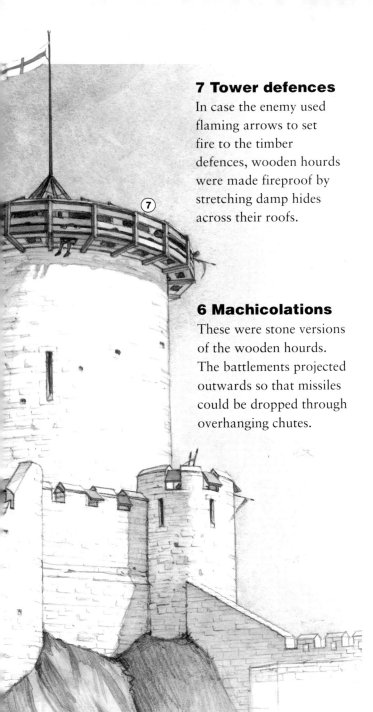

7 Tower defences

In case the enemy used flaming arrows to set fire to the timber defences, wooden hourds were made fireproof by stretching damp hides across their roofs.

6 Machicolations

These were stone versions of the wooden hourds. The battlements projected outwards so that missiles could be dropped through overhanging chutes.

4 Portcullis

The portcullis slid down grooves in the stone walls. It was fixed to ropes and was operated by winding gear in the upper part of the gatehouse.

5 The barbican

The barbican was a walled area in front of the inner gatehouse. If an enemy reached it, he would be fired at on all sides by the castle defenders.

Castle defences

Many castles were built on high ground with clear views of the surrounding countryside so a surprise attack was out of the question. As an enemy attacker neared the castle, its massive walls and towers would loom menacingly above him. The only entrance was through a terrifying outer gatehouse, behind which was a barbican protecting the inner gate. Even if an attacker broke through this set of defences, there were more gates, walls and towers to overcome before the castle could be captured.

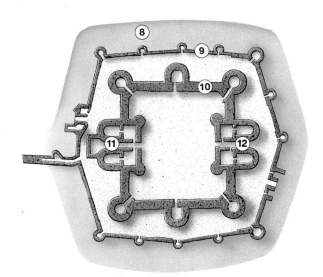

Beaumaris Castle

Beaumaris Castle in Wales was designed so that there were no weak points. This plan shows its moat (8), outer walls (9), inner walls (10) and two huge gatehouses (11 and 12). Building began in 1295 but was never completed.

CASTLE LIFE

Most castles were built for living in as well as for defence. Kings often owned many castles, and lords and other powerful knights might own several, travelling from one to another. Lesser knights often lived in smaller fortified manor houses which were still large enough to include a great hall and often a chapel.

A child's life

Children had chores to help with around the house, and some lessons.

But they would also play with their toys, such as wooden knights operated by strings. Games included hoodman blind, a game of tag like Blindman's Bluff.

▶ **This is a manor house in England, built in the 12th century but added to over the next 400 years. It is a large country house rather than a castle, but has a moat and is fortified against attacks.**

Home comforts

In the early Middle Ages castles and houses were often cold and damp. Smoky fires burned in the middle of the room, but there were few chimneys. Glass was a luxury – most windows had iron bars and shutters. So letting in light meant letting in the wind. Waste from garderobes, or toilets, dropped into the moat or a cesspit. During the 15th century, life became more comfortable.

Knights shared their busy lives with their families, with pages and squires, soldiers, priests, servants, cooks and grooms. Much of the management was carried out by the lady of the castle, or châtelaine, especially when the knight was away. Children would have the run of the castle, rushing around the battlements on warm summer evenings, getting in the way of the grooms in the stables, or being chased from the kitchens. In winter, with snow lying on the ground, the children would huddle by the log fire in the draughty solar, or private living room, while their mother embroidered and told them tales.

KEY

1 great hall	6 solar (private living room)
2 kitchens	7 passage
3 scullery	8 keep
4 bedchambers	9 stables
5 garderobe (toilet)	10 gatehouse
	11 moat

▼ In northern Italy, noble families often lived in towns rather than in castles. However they still needed to defend themselves, so they built tall stone towers. San Gimignano, in the Italian region of Tuscany, still has 13 medieval towers. At one time there were 76 of them!

Food and drink

 Most castles kept only a small amount of food in storage all year round. But when the king or lord visited, the courtyard would ring with commands and curses and the clatter of rolling barrels. Servants filled the cellars and storerooms with sides of salty bacon and heavy sacks of grain and flour. The steward would check old supplies to make sure that the grain for making bread had not gone mouldy, or the wine had not turned sour.

barley

rye

wheat

Preserving food

Although a castle's stone cellars were cool, it was impossible to keep food fresh for long. Most meat was therefore smoked or heavily salted so that it would last through the winter. Vegetables were dried or pickled.

Sometimes, layers of fruit and meat were stored together in barrels. The fruit juices soaked into the meat and helped to preserve it. This is where the word 'mincemeat' (the sweet fruit mixture put into pies at Christmas) comes from.

Mushrooms and onions (1) were often threaded on long strings and hung up to dry.

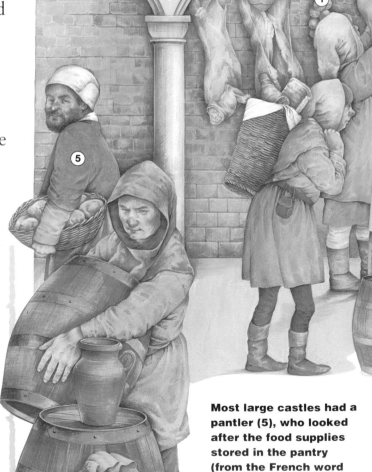

Daily bread

Before baking bread, grain such as barley, rye and wheat had to be ground into flour. Some castles had their own windmills which were built high on the castle or town walls. There, the windmill's sails would catch the wind and turn the heavy grinding stones inside.

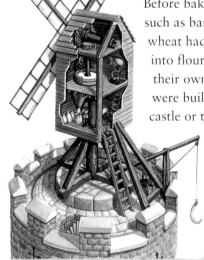

Most large castles had a pantler (5), who looked after the food supplies stored in the pantry (from the French word *painetterie*, meaning bread store).

White meats

Milk from sheep, goats and cows, and the cream, butter and cheese made from it, were called 'white meats'. The creamiest part of the milk was made into soft cheese or butter for the lord

and his family. Servants had to make do with a thick, hard cheese made from the rest of the milk. Sometimes, this cheese was so tough it had to be smashed into pieces with a hammer before it could be eaten!

Meat was salted in a salting box (2). Then it was hung on huge hooks (3) or stored in barrels (4).

Well water

Every castle needed its own supply of fresh water – especially if it was to survive a siege. Deep stone-lined shafts were dug to underground springs and the water was raised in wooden buckets using a rope and a windlass. Sometimes water was channelled straight to the kitchens.

Special jobs

Some jobs carried great honour and importance. The butler looked after the castle's supplies of wine, and the ewerer made sure that the lord's tablecloths and napkins were always clean. Both these jobs were done by noblemen who were chosen by the lord.

ewerer

butler

As sweet as honey

Some castles kept honey bees. Honey was used to sweeten food and drink. It was also one of the main ingredients in mead – a strong alcoholic drink popular during the Middle Ages.

Larger castles had their own fishponds, orchards and vine-yards, as well as gardens which supplied vegetables and herbs. Cattle, sheep and pigs were kept on surrounding farmlands. The lord's hunting parties also brought back deer, wild boar and pheasants from the forests for special feasts.

35

The kitchen

When the lord was away, the castle kitchen was quiet. The constable might eat alone in his private room, and a small garrison needed only basic meals. However, during the lord's visit, the kitchen buzzed with activity. The cook bellowed orders and the under-cooks chopped vegetables, plucked poultry and pounded meat until it was tender. The worst jobs in the kitchen, such as cleaning the cauldron or fetching water from the well, were done by young boys called scullions.

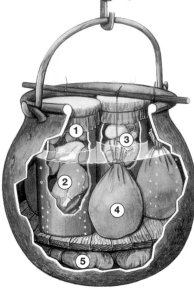

adjustable pot-hook

Spice it up

Food was often heavily spiced, which helped to disguise the taste of rotten meat! Many spices came from the Middle and Far East. They were very expensive so only the rich could afford them.

Cauldron cooking

All kitchens had at least one big iron cauldron which was slung on a hook over an open fire. Cauldrons were used for stews, soups and sauces. Sometimes, they were packed with several dishes, all to be cooked at once – shown here: eggs (1), chickens (2) and fish (3), in sealed pottery jars, puddings in cloth bags (4), and a slab of bacon (5).

ginger

nutmeg

cardamon

cinnamon

▼ Pots and plates were cleaned with sand or with soapy herbs like soapwort. Dirty water was poured away through a sink built into an outside wall.

Kitchen tools

Important kitchen tools included a pestle and mortar (1) for grinding up spices and herbs, a stirring stick (2), a meat pounder (3), a metal skimmer for soups (4), and various knives for chopping up vegetables and meat (5).

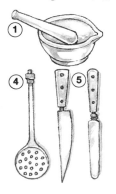

The warmest part of the kitchen was in front of the blazing hearth. Here, a scullion called a 'turnspit' had the hot and sweaty job of turning a long pole on which meat was skewered for roasting. A dome-shaped oven for baking bread was usually built into the side of the hearth. It was heated with blazing brushwood and stayed hot for hours.

Multi-coloured food
Food was not only spicy, it was also coloured with vegetable dyes and sometimes gilded with gold. Parsley was used for green, saffron for yellow and sandalwood for red.

The great hall

On special occasions magnificent banquets were held in the castle's great hall. The lord, his family and the most important guests sat at the high table, which was raised above the other diners and covered with a tablecloth of the finest linen. A gold or silver boat-shaped ornament called a nef was placed in the middle of the table and was used to hold the lord's napkin.

▶ The cup-bearer stood to the left of the lord. He made sure that the lord's cup was always filled with wine.

Table manners

At meals, there were rules about how to behave when eating. Just like today, it was thought rude to talk with your mouth full or to munch noisily as you ate.

◀ Some lords didn't care much about fine table manners!

After a fanfare of trumpets sounded, a procession of servants brought in the dishes. Guests might be offered soups and jellies, eels and lampreys, roast goose, heron or swan, huge pies and fruit tarts. The food was served up in dishes called messes which were shared between several people. Honoured guests had their own messes and ate off gold or silver plates. Everyone else used a trencher – a big slice of stale bread which soaked up the grease from the food. Leftovers were saved for the poor waiting at the castle gates.

▲ An aquamanile held water for washing hands before each meal. The water was poured out through a spout in the top.

An early start
Banquets and other formal meals began early – at about 10 or 11 in the morning – and lasted for several hours.

Polite company
Guests with good manners would share cups of wine and offer food from their own plates to a neighbour.

Guests ate with their fingers or with knives or spoons. Forks were not used until the end of the Middle Ages.

▶ Food was soft and mushy so it could be scooped up on to bread, or it was carved into small pieces so it could be picked up by a knife.

Home life

In early castles, life was far from comfortable. The wind whistled through wooden shutters in the windows and most people slept on benches or on rough mattresses in the great hall. But by the 1200s, castles had well-furnished bed chambers and living rooms, heated by large open fires and lit by candles. The better rooms had glass windows and plastered walls hung with fine tapestries. Floors were covered with sweet-smelling herbs or rush matting.

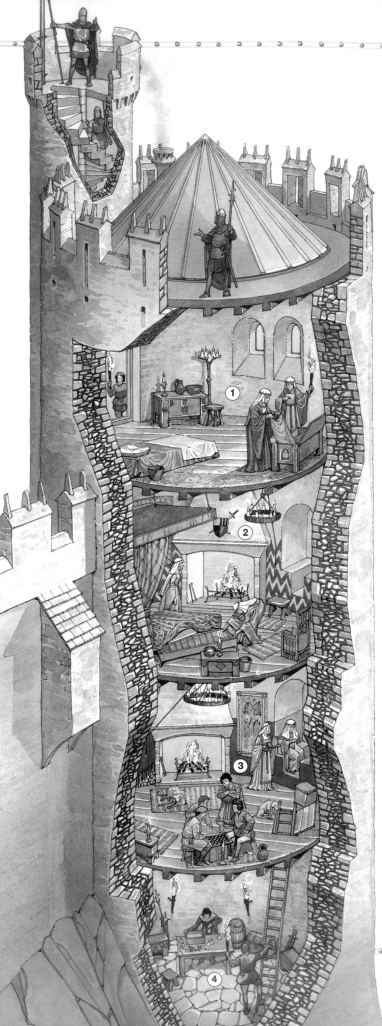

1 The wardrobe
The top room in the lord's tower was used by the lady's personal servants. Linen and clothes were stored in large chests.

2 Master bedroom
This had rush mats on the floor and richly decorated walls. A lady-in-waiting could sleep on the truckle bed which was pulled out from under the main bed.

3 The solar
This was the lord's private living room. After a hearty meal he might retire here for a game of chess.

4 Basement
A trapdoor from the solar led down to the basement. Weapons, coins and other valuables might have been kept here.

Reading and writing

Few people in the Middle Ages knew how to read and write. There were not many schools and most children never went to one. Boys had more opportunity to learn than girls, but there were still some famous women writers, such as Christine de Pisan, who lived in France in the 1400s.

Entertainment

Travelling musicians called jongleurs often visited the castle to entertain guests. Lords and ladies also liked to play music, sing and compose poetry themselves. Listening to storytellers' tales of romance and chivalry, embroidery and games of chess were other popular pastimes.

harpist

lute-player

The lady, the wife of the lord, usually played an important part in running the castle. She organized the servants and entertained visiting noblewomen. When the lord was away, she might inspect local farms or organize supplies and repairs to the castle. Even so, this was still a man's world. It was believed that women were inferior to men and, in some areas, they could not own land or make a will.

Married young

Many marriages between nobles were arranged when the children were still in their cradles, and most lords and ladies were married by the time they were fourteen.

Growing up

From the age of six or seven, the children of nobles were often sent to live in another lord's castle. Boys became pages and learned how to fight. Girls learned how to manage a household.

► Toilets were sometimes built on different floors, one above the other. The topmost one was often in the open air.

▲ A green baize cloth with a hole cut in the middle helped to warm up the cold stone seat.

▼ Waste from the garderobes dropped down into the moat or into a special pit.

Clean and healthy

People in the Middle Ages were much less fussy about living in smelly and dirty places than we are today. A castle's toilets were little more than holes with stone seats, few rooms had running water, and baths were an expensive luxury. Every now and then the castle was cleaned from top to bottom. Wisely, the lord and lady would leave for a week or two while the whole building was aired, scrubbed and swept. The horrible job of cleaning out the cesspits below the toilets was done by men called 'gong farmers'.

Garderobes

The lord sometimes had his own private toilet, or garderobe, next to his chambers. Torn strips of linen were used instead of toilet paper, and sweet-smelling herbs were sprinkled on the floor.

Rats, rats, rats

Rats were everywhere – in the kitchens, in the cellars, in the stables... Rats destroyed stores of grain and spread diseases. They carried the fleas which spread the deadly sickness called the plague.

Bathtime

Only the richest people could enjoy a soak in a hot bath. Wood for heating the water, cloth to line the tub, and bath oils all had to be paid for. King John of England bathed once a month and it cost him five pence each time. (A labourer had to work a whole week to earn this amount.)

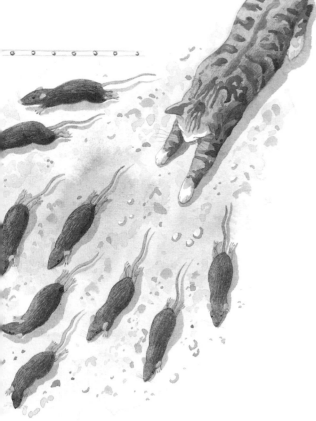

Herbal remedies

In the Middle Ages, doctors often used herbs to treat their patients. Comfrey was meant to help broken bones mend quickly. Yarrow was applied to flesh wounds to help stop any bleeding.

Between 1347 and 1351 a plague known as the Black Death killed about 25 million people in Europe and Asia. People knew nothing about the germs which spread disease. Young women died giving birth and young men died of wounds they received in battle. But if people escaped these disasters, they often lived to a ripe old age.

▼ Apart from ladies-in-waiting, laundresses were the only other women who worked in the castle. The rest of the jobs were done by men and boys.

Making soap

Soap made from olive oil and scented with herbs was used in southern Europe from the 700s but was not widely available in northern Europe until much later. Often, soap was made locally from animal fat, wood ash and soda.

► Folded clothes and bedding were put into a barrel and liquid soap was poured through them. Then they were pounded with a wooden bat to remove the dirt.

Keeping in fashion

Fashion was very important in the Middle Ages. Just as kings built huge castles to impress people, the wealthy dressed in rich costumes to impress each other. On important occasions noblemen and noblewomen wore jewels and gold chains and brightly coloured clothes. Colours had different meanings. Blue meant you were in love, yellow meant anger and grey meant sadness.

◄ Women often hid their hair beneath head-dresses. Some of these were shaped like animal horns and others like butterflies' wings.

► The 'steeple hat' or hennin could be nearly a metre tall! It needed a wire frame inside to support it.

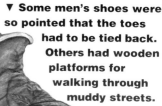

▼ Some men's shoes were so pointed that the toes had to be tied back. Others had wooden platforms for walking through muddy streets.

Trendsetters

In the early 1400s, the well-dressed nobleman might wear a hat with a tail called a 'liripipe' which draped over his shoulder (1). In the 1450s, knee-length clothes lined with fur (2) became popular with the nobles while merchants wore longer robes (3). Women's dresses often had long trains which had to be looped over the arm (4) and hats were very tall (5). Short tunics and pointed shoes (6) were all the rage with the most fashionable young men.

Working clothes

Peasants could not afford to buy fancy clothes. Instead, they wore simple tunics and shifts, woollen stockings, cloaks, straw hats, hoods and caps. With frequent repairing, these clothes could last for many years.

In the early Middle Ages, the rich wore fairly simple clothes. But from the 1100s, fashions became more and more elaborate. Just like today, fashions, including hats, shoes, hairstyles, tunics and coats, varied from year to year. Laws banning outrageous dress were passed in many parts of Europe in the 1200s and 1300s but they were usually ignored.

▼ There were no shops selling ready-made clothes so the rich paid tailors to make the latest fashions.

The chapel

Most castles had a small private chapel near to the lord's chambers. Painted walls, stained-glass windows and a golden cross on the altar made it the castle's most beautiful room. The lord and lady began each day by attending a short service here. Some castles also had a larger chapel in the courtyard for the other castle residents.

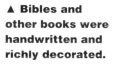

▲ **Bibles and other books were handwritten and richly decorated.**

Prayer time

Religious ceremonies in the castle's chapel were performed by the priest. He also said grace before the beginning of every meal, thanking God for the food about to be eaten. Priests were one of the few people in the castle who could read and write. They were often put in charge of castle documents.

Holy days

Religious festivals were an important part of everyday life. They were celebrated with public holidays when everybody took the day off work. Sometimes, travelling actors performed mystery and miracle plays in front of a church or cathedral. These showed well-known stories from the Bible, or the lives of saints.

► **Other entertainers often tried to lure away a play's audience!**

▼ **Pilgrims who had been to Santiago de Compostela wore cockleshells in their hats.**

▼ **Dishonest relic-sellers sold wooden crosses which, they claimed, were made from the cross on which Jesus Christ was crucified.**

relic seller

nun

pilgrim

bishop   monk

During the Middle Ages, most people were very religious. Many Christians proved their faith by going on pilgrimages. They travelled huge distances to visit holy places such as Rome, Jerusalem and Santiago de Compostela in Spain. Others became monks or nuns and lived in abbeys, monasteries or convents. Here, they spent their lives in prayer, copying out the scriptures or helping the sick.

Hunting and hawking

The best-loved sport was hunting and most lords kept special horses for hunting game. The horses were well cared for and often led a better life than the servants who looked after them! Hunting dogs were also highly valued. They were specially trained to sniff out and track down their prey. Every king and lord usually had a favourite hound which followed him about the castle. The dogs were looked after by the lord's huntsmen and kennel-grooms.

▲ This scene shows a pack of hunting dogs catching a wild boar. Dogs wore collars to protect their throats in case the boar tried to gore them with its sharp tusks.

The hunt
Some of the animals hunted by the nobles included deer, wild boar, wolves, foxes and bears. But hunting was more than just a sport. It also provided meat for the dinner table.

Falconry

Birds of prey were the most prized of all hunting animals. It took time and great skill to train them to catch smaller birds, hares and rabbits. The type of bird you hunted with depended on your rank in society – an emperor hunted with an eagle, a king or queen with a gyrfalcon, a lord with a peregrine falcon and a noblewoman with a hawk Birds of prey were kept in a long wooden shed called a mews and were looked after by the falconer.

► **A falconer wore a gauntlet to protect his hand from the bird's sharp claws.**

In the early Middle Ages, Europe had huge forests which teemed with deer, wild boar, foxes and bears. But over the years, large areas of woodland were cut down and turned into farmland. By the 1100s, some areas were set aside just for hunting. These were called royal forests and any peasants found poaching game from them faced harsh punishment. If they were caught they might be blinded or even killed, but many still tried to catch a hare or squirrel for the pot.

Falconry kit

Special equipment was used to train and look after birds of prey. A leash stopped a bird flying away, bells helped to find a lost bird, a hood kept it calm, and a leather purse might contain a tasty reward.

leash

bells

hood

purse

A test of honour

Often at tournaments, the helmets of the competitors were first shown to the ladies of the court. The ladies pointed out if any of the knights concerned had offended against the rules of chivalry – he might have been rude about one of them. If so, the knight could be banned from the festivities.

Grandstands were set up around the ground, which was decorated with banners and coats-of-arms. The watching nobles and retainers became excited. Sometimes violence broke out among competitors and spectators, so they were searched for concealed weapons before the tournament.

▼ With the development of tournaments, the knights' armour became more decorative. Here the fancy crests identify the knights.

The tournament

Over 800 years ago, knights began to fight mock battles as a team sport. This gave them a chance to practise fighting and to show off their skills. The first contests were rough free-for-alls, known as mêlées. Soon all kinds of rules were drawn up. As the idea of chivalry spread around Europe, tournaments became more and more popular.

Jousting

Jousting armour became increasingly specialized. For example, a knight had to crouch forward for the charge in order to see out of the 'frog-mouthed' helm. On impact he straightened up and the helmet covered his eyes. The armour's left side was reinforced since the knights passed left side to left side and so received the blows there.

frogmouthed helm

tilt

▼ **The ladies of court, dressed in their finest clothes, looked on admiringly. A knight would declare himself a favourite lady's champion, wearing her scarf on his sleeve.**

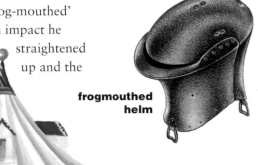

Tournaments offered a chance for young knights to make a name for themselves, which could sometimes lead to a profitable marriage. Knights travelled from one country to another in search of glory. The most popular one-to-one fight was the joust, a horseback charge with lances, in which each knight tried to knock the other to the ground. From the 1420s, the two riders were separated by a fence called a tilt. Prizes such as armour or gold were awarded to the winner.

◄ **The tournament was a colourful pageant, but a dangerous one. Although blunted or wooden weapons were introduced, injuries and even deaths were common.**

READY FOR BATTLE

The knight had to make sure that his weapons and armour were kept in good condition. At any time he might receive a summons to war from his lord or from the king himself. Sometimes it was possible to pay money instead of fighting, but one day he would have to ride to war. He would probably take with him retainers, a small band of local men. These might include his squire, several men-at-arms (mounted soldiers), and footsoldiers or archers. They would join other troops, under the standard of a commander, or knight banneret.

armour mark from Milan

◄ This statue of 1480 from Venice shows an Italian knight called Bartolomeo Colleoni riding to war. He was a condottiere, or mercenary, a knight who was contracted to fight for money rather than as a feudal duty.

▼ A small armourer's workshop would be crowded with master craftsmen and with apprentices learning the trade. Lengths of iron bar were hammered out into sheets and then cut to a pattern with powerful shears. The metal was hammered into shape over anvils and stakes. It could be strengthened by processes of heating and cooling. The finished pieces were then polished and lined with canvas that was sewn to a leather strip and padded with straw.

Buying armour

If a knight wished to survive a campaign, he would need to buy a good and often very expensive suit of armour. Low-grade armour was made and repaired all over Europe. But metalwork of the very best quality tended to come from workshops in Italian cities such as Milan and Brescia, or from southern German cities such as Augsburg and Nuremberg, which had access to plentiful supplies of iron ore and charcoal. Rich knights from Britain or France might send an order to one of these centres. Suits could be purchased ready-made, or specially fitted.

A coat of mail

A knight leaves for war in the 1100s, wearing mail armour. His long tunic is called a byrnie or hauberk. This comes down to the knees, where it is slit so that he can mount his horse more easily. The mail hood protecting the neck below the helmet is called a coif. Underneath the mail, the knight wears a padded garment called an aketon. This word comes from *al-qutum*, the Arabic for cotton.

Helmets

In the 11th and 12th centuries, most knights wore a cone-shaped helmet with a nose-bar, or nasal. By the end of the 12th century, guards for the whole face appeared, and then the helm, which covered the whole head. The basinet of the 14th century included a visor, which could be raised. The fanciest helmets of all were made for tournaments.

Armour

The first medieval knights rode into battle in mail. This was a tough metal fabric which could bend easily because it was made up of interlinking iron rings. The fabric was shaped so that it fitted well, covering the head and forming a heavy tunic over the body. Mail didn't offer complete protection – it could be pierced by arrows or weapons. From the late 13th century, knights began to cover their knees with steel plates, and in the next 100 years more plates were added.

▼ Great helm, developed in the early 13th century. This one dates from *c.* 1250, but after the 14th century they were mostly used for jousting.

crest of stuffed leather

nasal

leather chin strap

▲ Conical helmet, 11th and early 12th century

rivets attaching canvas and padded lining

aventail, or removable neck guard

side-pivoting visor

▲ Basinet from Italy, from late 14th to early 15th century

▲ Barbute from Italy, *c.* 1445

► Gold etched jousting helmet from northern Italy, *c.* 1570

A trusty shield

The knight's shield protected him from showers of arrows and deadly weapon thrusts. It could also be used to deal heavy blows. The design changed over the years from the long kite shield of the Normans to the smaller triangle shape of the 14th century, made of leather-covered wood. Plate armour made shields unnecessary.

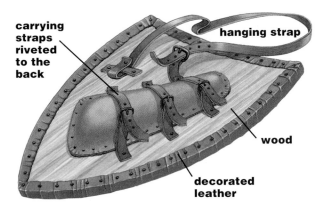

carrying straps riveted to the back

hanging strap

wood

decorated leather

By the 1400s, the knight's body was covered in tough plates of steel. These were well fitted and made up of sections joined by rivets and straps of leather. It cannot have been easy to fight in plate armour weighing about 25 kilograms. However, it was light enough for a knight to move quickly and get up if he fell from his horse.

▶ A squire removes the plate armour of a wounded knight in the 1400s. This was made of silvery steel. Mail was now worn only as part of the undershirt, or arming doublet, to which the plate was fastened with waxed points, or laces. In the 16th century new tactics and firearms changed the nature of warfare. Charging knights were less deadly than men with long pikes, and a suit of armour was not much protection against handguns.

1 helmet
2 bevor
3 breastplate
4 pauldron
5 besagew
6 vambrace
7 gauntlet
8 cuisse
9 greave
10 sabaton
11 arming doublet
12 waxed points
13 mail gusset

Deadly weapons

The sword, a symbol of knighthood, was cared for and kept near at hand in its scabbard, even during peacetime. King Arthur's legendary sword was called Excalibur, and many knights also gave their sword a special name. A typical European sword of the 12th century had a broad, flat, two-edged slashing blade, with a groove down the centre. By the 14th century, the increasing use of plate armour meant that a knight now had to force the blade through chinks and gaps.

Bows and arrows

Powerful crossbows could shoot 200 metres with their bolts, or quarrels, which were short-vaned iron-tipped darts. Increasingly a mechanism was used to help wind back the gut bowstring. The longbow was simpler to use, but pulling it needed great strength. It could be shot up to six times a minute (compared to once a minute for the crossbow). The metal-tipped arrows were over 75 centimetres long.

goose feather fletchings

longbow

various metal arrowheads

quarrel

crossbow 1400s

handgun 1400s

▶ A knight used a lance for charging into battle. This long wooden spear, tipped with steel, could strike at a distance, knocking the enemy off his horse. Crushing blows could be dealt out with an axe, a hammer or a mace, a kind of club often with a ridged metal head. The flail was a kind of club, which had iron balls fixed to a chain. Caltrops were iron spikes thrown to the ground to lame horses and men.

As battle began, the sky darkened with flight after flight of hissing arrows. Horses reared up as enemy soldiers raised pollaxes, blades set on long shafts. One medieval tale, the *Song of Roland*, describes weapons being used at close quarters. Skulls crack, brains are splattered and bodies are hacked to bits. All that counts in battle, says the hero, is iron and steel.

caltrop

dagger 1300s

lance c. 1100s

mace 1300s

pollaxe c. 1500s

great sword 1400s

sword 1300s

falchion 1200s

flail 1500s

Swords of this period were designed for stabbing and thrusting. The blades became narrower, sharply-pointed and no longer flat. There was a variety of types to suit the conditions: a dagger or a short sword called a baselard, for stabbing at close quarters; a great sword up to 1.2 metres long, so heavy that it had to be swung with both hands on the hilt; and a broad-bladed, single-edged chopping sword called a falchion.

Battling beasts

Horses played an important part in a knight's life. Except for the occasions when he dismounted to fight on foot, the knight's horse really was his key to survival in battle. It brought him into close contact with his enemy, and it allowed him to make his escape. It could even fight for him, rearing up and lashing out with its great hooves.

▶ Pack horses were used for carrying an army's baggage. The knight and his men used the best riding horses they could find. The finest warhorses, or destriers, were bigger and stronger.

Carrier pigeons

During the Crusades, Saracen armies used pigeons to carry secret messages from one city or army to another, and the Christians copied them. Pigeons were sometimes killed by trained falcons.

sumpter (packhorse)

Breeding the best

Mares and stallions of the best quality were set aside for breeding. Their foals were raised and trained for battles and tournaments. The warhorse had to be a stallion, large, powerful and lively, yet obedient to its master. In battle, a knight and his horse had to act together, perfectly co-ordinated despite the danger, noise and turmoil around them. The knight's squire led the horse by the right hand, so it became known as a destrier, an old word meaning 'right-hander'. Buying a destrier was very costly, and so was keeping it groomed and fed.

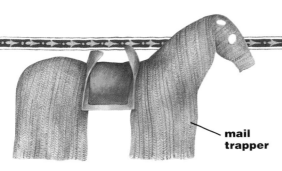

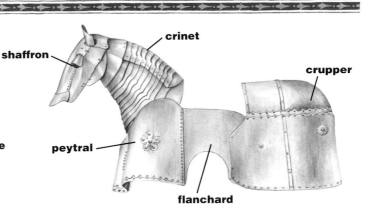

shaffron

crinet

crupper

peytral

flanchard

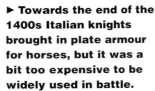

▲ Special armour called a bard was designed for horses. This was originally a covering called a trapper, made of lined cloth or mail.

► Towards the end of the 1400s Italian knights brought in plate armour for horses, but it was a bit too expensive to be widely used in battle.

hackney or nag (riding horse)

destrier (war horse)

palfrey (quality riding horse)

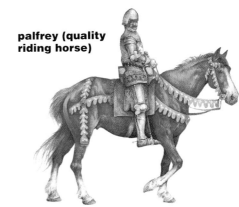

The saddle provided the solid platform from which the knight fought. It was often made of beechwood and covered with leather, and had high supports, or bows, at the front and back. The rider's legs were normally stretched out in the stirrups to steady himself, and on his heels he wore spurs, metal spikes to prod the horse into a gallop. By the 1240s, a wheel of spikes called a rowel was sometimes fitted to spurs. The knight carried the reins in his left hand. Perfect control of the horse was needed to keep in formation during the charge.

► A Knight Templar gives a lift to his comrade, who rides behind him. This badge showed that the order had humble origins – the two founding knights had only one horse between them.

War dogs

Fierce dogs called mastiffs were bred for keeping watch and guarding supplies in battle camps. Sometimes they were also used to attack the enemy's soldiers.

Open battle

A marching army swarmed over the countryside. The soldiers killed the peasants and burned anything that could be used by the enemy. Some knights rode ahead to find out the enemy's position and strength. Straggling out behind the army were supply wagons, followers and sick or wounded men. The leaders on each side planned how to trap the enemy, or sometimes how to avoid battle. Bad weather, the lie of the land, the risk of treachery and hunger all played a part in their decisions.

▲ This is how the fighting groups, or battalions, were drawn up for the Battle of Poitiers, in France, on September 19, 1356. Welsh archers positioned in the woods destroyed the opening charge of French knights. The remaining French knights joined battle on foot and were killed in their thousands. The Black Prince then sent a group to attack the French from the rear. Some of the French saved themselves by retreating.

Defences were hastily prepared by digging in stakes or by strewing the ground with metal spikes. As the troops were drawn up, they prayed for their lives and shouted support for their side. Battle often opened with a charge by the knights who, with their horses, were targetted mercilessly by the archers. Then hand-to-hand fighting began, a hellish nightmare of mud and blood. Knights sometimes fought on foot, forming a dense wedge of armour and weapons. Battles could last from one to three days, though often the armies were close to each other for several days beforehand.

Life in camp

The army has set up camp and the hillsides are dotted with fires and the colourful tents of the knights. Common soldiers scour the local countryside for food.

Preparing defences

The archers hammer pointed stakes into the ground, to protect themselves against a charge by the enemy knights. They line up behind the stakes. By this time the enemy army is very close by.

After the battle

Thousands might die in a single battle. Most of the wounded would be put out of their misery by a dagger or sword thrust, but some would crawl off to be bandaged by friends, or by monks and nuns.

◄ In 1356 Edward the 'Black Prince' raided France with 8,000 English and Gascons. Near Poitiers, he was drawn into open battle. Although outnumbered two to one, his army captured the French king and won the battle. The French fought bravely. Nearly 2,500 of their nobles may have been killed – possibly more than the number who were captured.

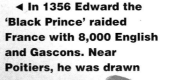

Capture and ransom

During a battle or siege, armies would try to capture as many enemy knights as possible. The prisoners were not normally killed – they were ransomed. This meant that they were held captive until a fee was received. The ransom might be paid by a knight's family or friends. Some ransoms were so high that a knight might remain captive for years – even for life.

▲ Christians captured in the Crusades are beheaded by the Saracens. During these 'holy' wars both sides tortured and killed large numbers of prisoners of war. When the Crusaders captured Jerusalem in 1099, the streets ran with the blood of the citizens. However, most victors preferred to charge ransom fees.

Knights as equals

One day two knights would be trying to kill each other in battle. The next they might be greeting each other politely, according to the rules of chivalry. Often knights felt that they had more in common with one another than with their own footsoldiers.

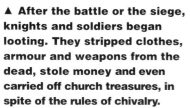

▲ After the battle or the siege, knights and soldiers began looting. They stripped clothes, armour and weapons from the dead, stole money and even carried off church treasures, in spite of the rules of chivalry.

▶ A captured knight was normally treated well. He might dine with his captors, play chess or go hunting.

A king's ransom was huge. In 1250 Louis IX of France was captured by Saracens during the Crusades. He agreed to surrender to them the Egyptian city of Damietta, and pay a vast amount of gold. In 1385 English troops, hired to fight for King John of Portugal, complained bitterly about losing their share of the money when the king did not ransom Castilian captives after the Battle of Aljubarrota. Only knights were worth ransoming. Common soldiers, who had no rich relatives, were simply killed, and the men, women and children of a captured town were often slaughtered too.

▲ The payment of ransoms could cause great hardship and bitterness back home. A vassal was expected to sell his lands in order to fund his lord's ransom. The people of England paid dearly in taxes when King Richard I, known as Coeur de Lion (Lionheart), was ransomed in 1193.

Freedom – at a price

The captured knight would probably be held in a castle, supervised by a knight called a constable. At last the money would arrive for his ransom and his release would be negotiated by a herald. Towards the end of the 12th century a religious order called the Trinitarians was founded in France. Their aim was to help organize the payment of ransoms for Christian knights captured in the Crusades.

Before settling down for a long siege, the commander might try to bribe the garrison to let him in, or poison the castle's water supply.

The commander's troops would then surround the castle, burn down the homes of the local people and cut off the castle's supply lines.

Wagons pulled by oxen would bring up the parts of the siege weapons so that they could be assembled nearer the castle walls.

A herald from the castle might come to discuss the terms of fighting.

Besieged!

 An enemy commander who wanted to capture a castle and the land around it had to plan his tactics carefully. Before beginning a siege, he took a good look at the countryside. Could the castle be easily surrounded? Where were its weak spots? Where would the siege weapons be most effective?

▲ In 1370, the English besieged the town of Troyes in France. This picture from the 1470s shows English heralds asking the French to surrender.

If the castle could not be taken quickly, the attackers aimed to starve the castle's garrison until they had to give in. In fact, few castles held out to the bitter end. The constable might only have to defend the castle for 40 days. If his lord or his king had not sent help by then, the constable could surrender to the enemy with honour.

Under attack

The battle is now on. The enemy has assembled their siege weapons – the trebuchet and the mangonel – and has begun hurling boulders and flaming missiles at the defences. The moat has been drained and filled with brushwood and earth. Soldiers clamber up a long scaling ladder that has been thrown against the wall, and the belfry has reached the battlements. The defenders shelter behind the wooden hourds or take cover in the embrasures behind the arrow loops, and return the enemy's fire.

1 Taking shelter
Crossbowmen and archers were protected from the castle defenders' fire by large wooden shields called pavises.

2 Filling the ditch
The ditch left after the moat had been drained was filled and boarded over so that the siege machines could be wheeled right up to the castle walls.

3 Battering ram
The soldiers pushing the battering ram against the castle gate were protected by a wooden frame covered in wet animal hides.

Undermining
Before castles had moats or once a moat had been drained, the attackers could dig their way under the castle's walls. They then lit a fire in the tunnel so that the timbers supporting its roof collapsed, along with the walls above.

4 Belfry
The belfry tower allowed the attackers to make a direct assault on the battlements.

5 Trebuchet
This giant catapult was powered by a heavy counterweight. A sling at the other end hurled rocks against the walls.

6 Mangonel
The mangonel was another kind of catapult powered by twisted ropes.

7 Cannons
Cannon barrels were raised or lowered on a heavy wooden beam.

End of a siege

The weeks pass by slowly. The attackers are tiring and the troops begin to mutter that they are wasting their time. If they haven't been able to batter down the walls, perhaps they can bribe their way in with offers of gold? The castle defenders have their own problems.

Food supplies are running out and water is strictly rationed. But then the defenders' luck changes – a look-out spies glinting armour in the distance. Help is less than a day's march away.

Cannon power

The first cannons were used in Europe during the early 1300s. They were poorly made and sometimes exploded in the faces of the gunners.

Over the years cannon design improved, but until the 1450s few were powerful enough to bring down a castle's walls.

▼ The most powerful cannons were called bombards. Some were over three metres long.

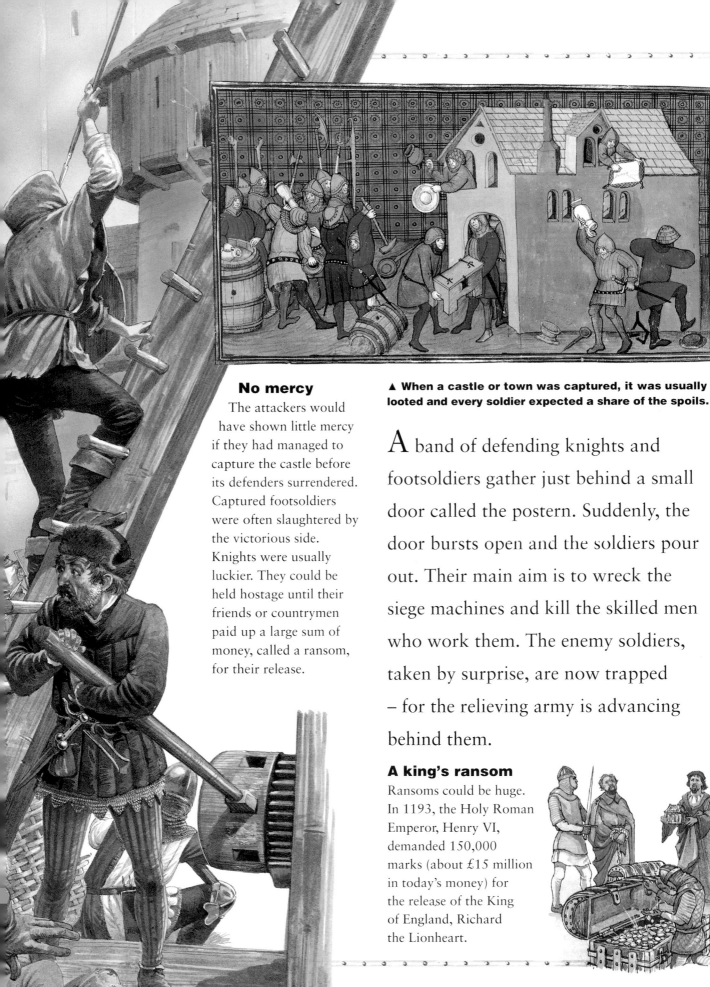

▲ When a castle or town was captured, it was usually looted and every soldier expected a share of the spoils.

No mercy

The attackers would have shown little mercy if they had managed to capture the castle before its defenders surrendered. Captured footsoldiers were often slaughtered by the victorious side. Knights were usually luckier. They could be held hostage until their friends or countrymen paid up a large sum of money, called a ransom, for their release.

A band of defending knights and footsoldiers gather just behind a small door called the postern. Suddenly, the door bursts open and the soldiers pour out. Their main aim is to wreck the siege machines and kill the skilled men who work them. The enemy soldiers, taken by surprise, are now trapped – for the relieving army is advancing behind them.

A king's ransom

Ransoms could be huge. In 1193, the Holy Roman Emperor, Henry VI, demanded 150,000 marks (about £15 million in today's money) for the release of the King of England, Richard the Lionheart.

The Moors, whose territory included north Africa, called their land in Spain al-Andalus. This was divided into taifas, or kingdoms. The reconquest of Spain by Christians began in the north in 727. Wars raged across Spain like wildfire during this time. They were not just simple conflicts between the Christian knights and the Moors. Moorish rulers fought amongst themselves and so did the Christian kings. The Christian knight El Cid was respected by both sides, and in 1081 he was hired to defend the Moslem kingdom of Saragossa.

▲ El Cid and his victorious knights took Valencia from the Moors in 1094, after many months' siege. El Cid became ruler of Valencia and the most famous knight in Spanish history. His nickname was taken from the Arabic al-Sayyid, meaning 'lord'. His real name was Rodrigo Díaz de Vivar.

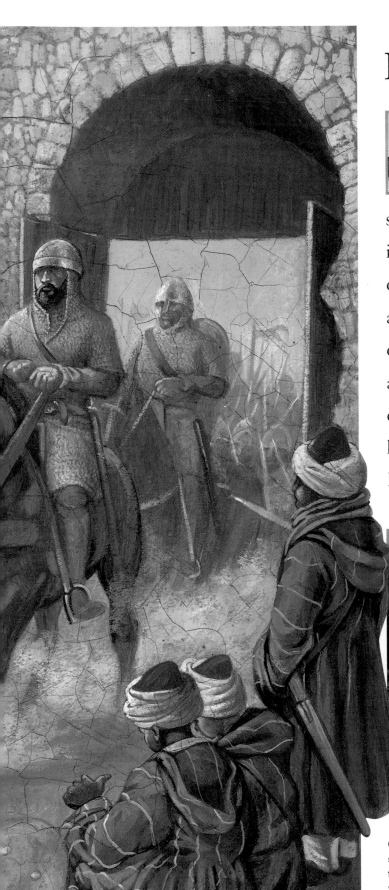

Fields of conflict

 Visitors come from all over the world to admire Europe's medieval towns – the narrow streets and the crooked houses, the impressive castles and the soaring spires of cathedrals. They easily forget that although life in the Middle Ages was often colourful and exciting, it could also be short and wretched. Many parts of Europe and southwest Asia became killing fields, torn apart by warfare for hundreds of years.

▲ The walls of the Alhambra tower above the city of Granada, in Spain. This site includes a massive fortress, the Alcazaba, as well as a beautiful palace, the Casa Real.

The Alhambra was built during the Middle Ages by Granada's Moslem rulers. When it was captured by the Christians in 1492, it marked the end of centuries of warfare with the Moors in Spain.

Holy wars

From 1096 wave after wave of Christian Crusaders invaded the 'Holy Land' of the Bible, then in Moslem hands. They were encouraged by popes and kings eager for new land and wealth. The Crusaders came from all over Europe, but in the east they were all known as 'Franks'. Most Crusaders were knights and soldiers, but ordinary people also set out hoping to gain God's approval. Many of them robbed and looted on the way, or were themselves killed.

Warriors of Islam

Saracen cavalryman

Like the Christian knights, many Saracen troops wore mail coats, or hauberks, as armour under their robes. Others were protected by quilted tunics or shirts made up of small steel plates. They carried fine swords and round shields. Turkish archers had short, powerful bows and shot arrows as they rode.

Knights of Outremer

The Crusaders captured Jerusalem in 1099. The lands they conquered became new Christian kingdoms, which together were known as Outremer ('overseas'). Many of the Christians who settled in these lands soon adopted the ways of the east.

As the Christian forces marched up the valley towards the waters of Lake Tiberias, they were hemmed in by Saladin's forces. These forces were in three divisions: Saladin himself; his brother Taqi al Din's troops; and Gökböri's division, all supported by a large number of followers and volunteers.

HATTIN July 4, 1187

Taqi al Din's division

Saracen volunteers

Count Raymond's division charges north to break through the Moslem troops and get to water

King Guy's division moves up under the Horns and try to make a defensive camp

Main Christian forces

Grass fires started by Saracens along the route of the Crusader troops' march

Christian rear

Gökböri's division

MEDITERRANEAN SEA

Damascus
Tyre
Acre Hattin
Nazareth Lake Tiberias
Belvoir
KINGDOM OF JERUSALEM
Jerusalem

The Crusader forces were made up of King Guy of Jerusalem in the centre, Count Raymond with the advance party, and the rearguard.

In the end some of the rearguard cavalry escape south past Gökböri's division

The Crusades may have been seen as 'holy' wars, but they brought lasting terror and misery to the Near East. There were eight major Crusades from 1096 to 1270. The knights' aims became more and more confused. In 1204 a band of Crusaders even turned aside to attack the ancient Christian city of Constantinople. In 1291 Moslems captured the city of Acre and the Holy Land was lost to the Christians forever.

The Horns (twin hills) of Hattin

Finally King Guy's exhausted knights lay down their arms and are captured

Saladin's division

▼ Both Crusaders and Saracens (a general name for Turks and Arabs) built castles in the Holy Land. These were massive fortresses, built as military bases rather than as places to live. They were forever being besieged and captured by one side and then the other. This is Belvoir Castle, built on a cliff above the Jordan valley.

Saladin

Salah-ed-din Yussuf ibn Ayub, who lived from 1137 to 1193, was the most famous Saracen. In Europe he was known as Saladin. Of Kurdish birth, he was a skilled general who became ruler of Egypt and Syria. He was wise and admired by some Christian knights for his chivalrous behaviour.

◄ In 1187 the Christian armies of Outremer faced Saladin's troops at Hattin, in the hills behind Lake Tiberias. It was a hot day and the Christians were short of water. When a holy relic, believed to be part of Jesus's cross, was captured by the enemy, panic broke out. Mown down by the Saracen archers and scorched by grass fires, thousands of Christian knights were killed.

Terrifying tartars

At St Mary's Church in Krakow, Poland, a trumpeter still plays once an hour in honour of the city's watchman, killed by a Tartar arrow. From 1237 to 1242 the Tartar armies, made up of Mongols and other central Asian peoples, swept through Russia, Ukraine, Poland and Hungary. Tartars were cruel soldiers and brilliant horsemen, feared wherever they rode.

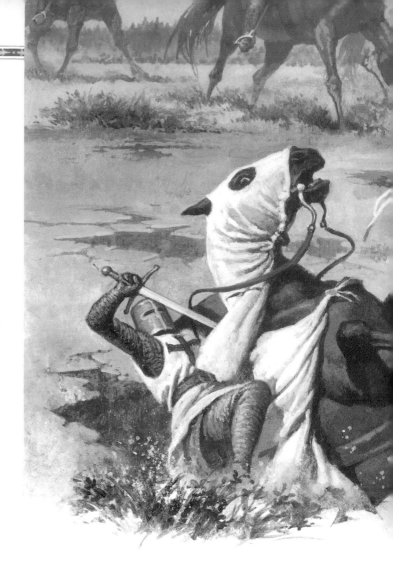

Riding east

Between 1150 and 1250, huge numbers of poor farmers and their families left the crowded lands of Holland and western Germany. They were seeking a new life in Prussia, Poland, Hungary and the Baltic lands. Joining them were their protectors, veteran knights of the great crusading orders such as the Teutonic Knights. They had a special mission, supported by the pope in Rome – to bring Christianity to the many non-believers who lived in eastern Europe.

▼ The Teutonic Knights called it Marienburg, while the Poles knew it as Malbork. This enormous castle, on the River Vistula near Gdansk, was begun in 1274. In 1309 it replaced Venice as headquarters of the Teutonic Order. The castle included three massive fortresses and a fine palace for the Grand Master of the Order.

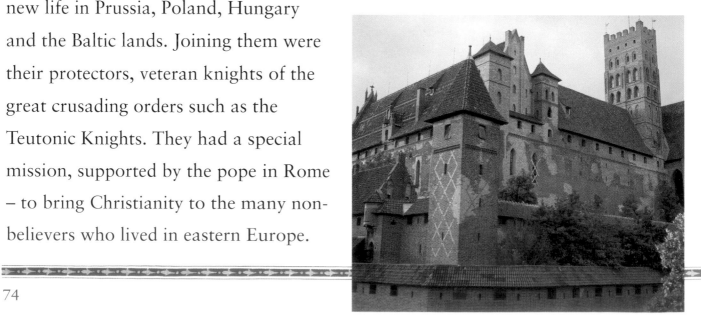

◄ On April 5, 1244, the Teutonic Knights charged across the frozen waters of Lake Peipus, on the eastern borders of Estonia. Their enemies were the Russians of Novgorod, led by Alexander 'Nevsky'. The Battle of the Ice lasted all day. The Teutonic Knights were slaughtered on the ice or drowned in the bitterly cold lake. Their attempt to win land and influence in Russia had been stopped.

The knights had other reasons for riding east besides this holy war. They were keen to defend the rich trading routes set up by the Hanse, a powerful alliance of merchant towns, and to win land and power. All went well and by the mid-14th century the Teutonic Order ruled a vast area of land around the Baltic Sea. However, in 1386 the kingdom of Poland united with Lithuania to the north and began to fight to reduce the power of the mighty Teutonic Order.

▼ On July 15, 1410, the knights of Poland, under King Wladislaw Jagiello, fought the Teutonic Order at Tannenberg, in Prussia. The Poles had originally invited the Teutonic Knights east to fight against the pagans. However, over the years the Poles had come to fear the Order, as it grew ever more powerful. At Tannenberg the Poles crushed the Teutonic Knights, killing over 200 of them, including the Grand Master Ulrich von Jungingen.

Killing fields

French was the international language of chivalry, courtly love and heraldry. However, France itself was fought over for centuries. Large areas of southwestern France were ruled by the English kings, who held land as Counts of Anjou. Although they were descended from Normans and spoke French, the English kings were at war with France until the end of the Hundred Years' War, a series of battles from 1338 to 1453. Year after year, English soldiers crossed the Channel to ravage France.

▼ In September 1415 an English army led by King Henry V landed near Harfleur in France. About 1,200 men stayed in the captured town, while 6,000 set out on a march to Calais. It was raining and conditions were bad. A French army was assembled to get rid of the raiders, and the two forces met at Agincourt.

▼ In 1358 two French knights, the Captal de Buch and the Count of Foix, were returning home from the wars in eastern Europe. Nearing Meaux, they heard that a jacquerie, or peasants' revolt, was in progress.

They entered the town with 25 other knights and their retainers, and slaughtered thousands of poorly armed rebels.

The English weren't the only problem. The state of Brittany was sometimes an ally of France and sometimes an enemy. In the 14th and 15th centuries eastern France, Luxembourg and Flanders all fell within the grasp of the Dukes of Burgundy. They had a deadly quarrel with the French kings, their close relatives, and fielded large armies which sometimes sided with England against the French.

Carcassonne

Burn the heretics!

In 1208 Pope Innocent III called for a new Crusade – not against Moslems but against fellow Christians living in southern France.

These 'Cathars' followed beliefs which were different from those of the Church, so they were sinful heretics. French knights in the north, eager for the spoils of war, hurried south. Thousands of Cathars were murdered. At the walled stronghold of Carcassonne many of them were captured and burned alive.

Agincourt

On October 25, 1415, French knights tried to block the English raiders in a muddy field outside the village of Agincourt. They failed and over 7,000 French troops were killed.

END OF AN AGE

About 500 years ago, knighthood was as popular as ever. Tournaments were in fashion and coats-of-arms were worn proudly. In battle, though, knights were powerless against cannon. Castles lay in ruins. More and more people worked for wages rather than as a feudal duty. States such as Spain, Portugal, England and France were ready to explore Asia and the 'New World' of the Americas. Western Europe was about to be torn apart by wars between the Church in Rome and the Protestants, who followed the teachings of a monk called Martin Luther. The age of knights was fading away.

Spanish Conquistadors in the New World

▼ **Constantinople is the city where Europe meets Asia. The city's fall to the forces of the Ottoman**

Turkish empire in 1453 put an end to the crusading ideals of knighthood.

Constantinople falls

On May 29, 1453, Moslem Turks entered Constantinople after a 52-day siege. This ancient city, known today as Istanbul, was the capital of the Christian Byzantine empire. It had been founded by the ancient Romans in AD 330. The fall of the city was a blow to Christendom and marked the last chapter of the Crusades.

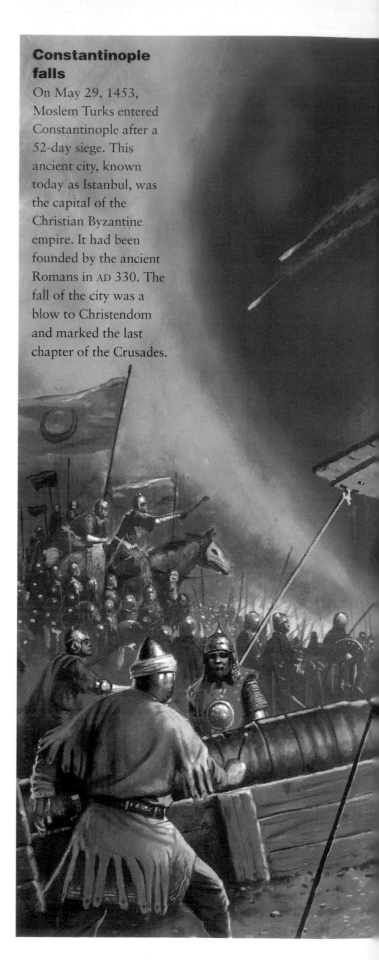

▼ In the late afternoon of May 28, 1453, an eerie hush hung over the city of Constantinople. Suddenly trumpets brayed and cymbals crashed. A vast army commanded by the Turkish sultan, Mehmed II, stood shouting before the walls of the city.

As sunset approached the archers on both sides exchanged deadly fire. Soon massive cannon were pounding the walls. Wave after wave of Turkish troops swarmed to the attack. The last Byzantine emperor, Constantine XI, died fighting.

The Christians dropped rocks over the walls and killed the enemy in their thousands, but the Turks kept on coming. At dawn on May 29th, the Turks marched in and raised their flags. Thousands of citizens were killed or sold into slavery.

Other knights

Were there knights in other countries or at other times? There were all kinds of mounted soldiers, but none quite like the knights of medieval Europe. Only in Japan, between the 10th and 19th centuries, might a knight have understood the way of life. Here there were soldiers with a code of honour and, from the 16th century, lofty castles too. Japanese knights called samurai (which like the English word 'knight' came from an old word meaning 'someone who serves') ranked high in society. They wore armour, carried swords and flew battle flags decorated with their lord's badges.

◄ Samurai, like European knights, were supported in battle by footsoldiers.

Samurai arms

The classic suit of Japanese armour was called o-yoroi or 'great armour'. It was made up of an iron breast-plate as well as shoulder guards and a skirt of small, lacquered metal plates. These were threaded together with silk. The samurai warrior was armed with a bow as well as with razor-sharp long and short swords. Samurai warriors fought for warlords and emperor.

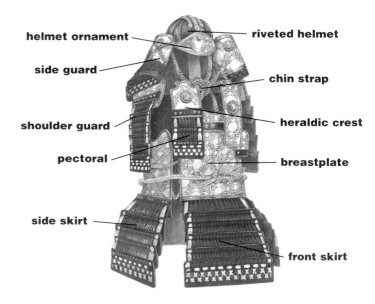

helmet ornament

riveted helmet

side guard

chin strap

shoulder guard

heraldic crest

pectoral

breastplate

side skirt

front skirt

◄ Han warrior 200 BC

Horsemen protected Chinese cities from raids by the fierce warriors of Central Asia.

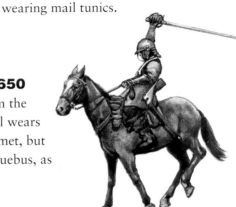

◄ Roman auxiliary AD 200

The Roman army included mounted cavalrymen wearing mail tunics.

► Gothic war chief AD 400

Fierce warriors from the north and east poured into southern Europe and smashed the Roman empire.

► English harquebusier 1650

This cavalryman from the English Civil War still wears a breastplate and helmet, but carries a gun, the arquebus, as well as his sword.

◄ Prussian officer 1815

At the time of the Battle of Waterloo, cavalry still fought with lances or swords.

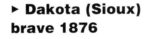

◄ Bengal lancer mid-1800s

Lancers formed an important part of mounted troops in India during the British empire.

► African cavalry 1820

Mounted warriors were used by powerful Islamic empires in the lands to the south of the Sahara desert.

► Dakota (Sioux) brave 1876

Young American Indians from the Great Plains formed élite warrior bands, who vowed never to retreat from battle.

◄ French cuirassier 1914

When World War I broke out, cavalry units faced guns and cannon.

► In September 1939 Poland was invaded from the west by Nazi Germany and from the east by the Soviet Union. The Polish cavalry rode into action armed with lances, just as their ancestors had at Tannenberg in 1410. However, lances were no defence against the tanks and aircraft of Blitzkrieg – 'lightning warfare'.

▲ This medieval French illustration shows the death of Roland, one of the finest knights at the court of the Emperor Charlemagne. The story of his fatal ambush in 778 was moved forward into the age of chivalry.

Tales of chivalry

The battles of the Middle Ages were mostly scenes of horror and misery, but we still tend to think of knights as heroes in shining armour. Like the real knights, we have been enchanted by tales of chivalry, honour and bravery. The stories of their day told of magic quests, tournaments and castles. Many of these were old tales rewritten in the language of chivalry.

Medieval stories

The Middle Ages were a time when many old stories and poems were being written down for the first time. A lot of these were tales that had been passed down by word of mouth for a thousand years or more. In the medieval versions, warriors and warlords were turned into chivalrous knights and kings, and pagan magic was converted into Christian miracles.

◄ Is this the Round Table of King Arthur's knights? No, it is a medieval fake from the 14th century. It was repainted in the 1480s and the 19th century. It hangs in Winchester.

► This picture shows noblemen staging a tournament – in 1839! At this time the Middle Ages came back into fashion. Painters sold pictures of knights and ladies. Some wealthy people even built fake castles to live in.

▲ In this Victorian painting from 1862, Sir Bedivere looks after the dying King Arthur. The real Arthur was probably a Celtic leader of the 6th century. Medieval writers turned him into a brave king attended by knights.

The tales go on...

Stories of Arthur and his knights started in Wales and Cornwall, and spread to Brittany. Minstrels took them on to France, Italy, England and Germany.

In 1470 a knight called Sir Thomas Malory wrote the *Morte d'Arthur* (the 'death of Arthur'). This inspired the poetry of Alfred, Lord Tennyson in the middle of the 19th century.

▲ In the *Song of the Nibelungs*, written in Germany about 800 years ago, ancient tales about a magical hero called Siegfried became mixed up with historical characters such as Attila the Hun. The old myths of the gods of the Germanic lands became a story of knighthood and chivalry, which in turn, in the middle of the 19th century, inspired four operas by Richard Wagner – the famous Ring Cycle.

CAMELOT.
RICHARD HARRIS · VANESSA REDGRAVE
FRANCO NERO · DAVID HEMMINGS
LIONEL JEFFRIES

▲ *Camelot* was a musical made into a film in 1967. It took its title from the court of King Arthur. The film was based on *The Once and Future King*, a series of wonderful stories by T H White.

▶ The legendary battles of English outlaw Robin Hood against the evil knights of the Sheriff of Nottingham have inspired countless books and films. This is *Robin Hood, Prince of Thieves* (1991).

▲ *Ivanhoe* was a very popular novel written by Sir Walter Scott and published in 1819. It was a tale of tournaments, Crusades and sieges. In the 1950s it was made into a film (above) and a television series.

Strangely, just as the real age of knights was passing away, people became more and more interested in tournaments and chivalrous stories. Jousts were still popular in the 17th and again in the 19th centuries. Even today, books, plays, films, television series and computer games return time after time to the subject of knights and chivalry – even if some of the tales are set in other worlds!

▼ Still fighting for truth and justice, Luke Skywalker takes on Darth Vader. The science-fiction film *Star Wars* (1977, 1997) is not so different from the old tales of knighthood, even if the swords are now laser-operated. Although it is over 500 years since the Middle Ages drew to a close, the ideals of chivalry have survived.

Castles in history

 Castle design changed greatly over the ages. Simple wooden towers surrounded by fences and ditches gave way to massive stone castles ringed by walls and moats. Later castles were more like palaces, designed for comfortable living rather than for protection and controlling land.

Time line

476 End of the Roman Empire in Europe.

700s Introduction of stirrups to Europe from Asia helps horsemen fight from the saddle.

800s Feudalism develops in western Europe.

950 Earliest known French castle built at Doué-la-Fontaine, Anjou.

1000s Chain mail armour worn by Normans.

stone keep

1066 William of Normandy invades England.

1080s Shell keeps built.

1096 Crusades begin.

1100s Stone keeps become the main castle stronghold. Crossbows and longbows in use.

1119 Order of Knights Templar founded.

1142 Crusaders take over Krak des Chevaliers in Syria.

▲ **1000s**
The first castles were made of wood. They stood on a mound called a motte. The outer enclosure was called a bailey.

motte

bailey

▶ This map, drawn in 1497, shows some of the most important castles stretching across the countries of Europe and North Africa.

1150-1250 Thousands of castles built across what is now Germany.

1180s Castles with square wall towers built.

1187 Jerusalem recaptured by Muslims.

1205 Krak des Chevaliers rebuilt by Knights Hospitaller.

1215 Signing of Magna Carta limits power of King of England.

◀ **1100s**
Soon stone was being used to build a massive stronghold or keep. This tower was the key to the whole castle's defence. Some keeps were square and some were round.

1220s Rounded wall towers begin to be built.

1270s Machicolations begin to replace wooden hourds.

1271 Krak des Chevaliers falls to Muslims.

1280s Edward I builds concentric castles in England and Wales.

1283 Conquest of Wales by Edward I.

1291 End of the Crusades.

1320s Cannons first used in battle.

1330 Plate armour in widespread use.

▼ **1290s**
Concentric castles relied on rings of walls, towers and strong gatehouses for their defence.

inner wall

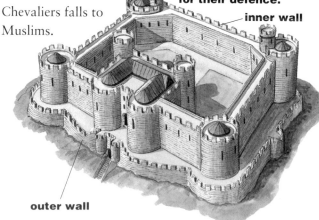

outer wall

1337 Start of Hundred Years War between England and France.

1347–51 Black Death kills 25 million people across Europe.

1350s Some castles in Britain and Holland built from brick.

1400 Welsh rise against the English.

Castles around the world

▼ Saumur Castle, in France, was re-built several times during the Middle Ages.

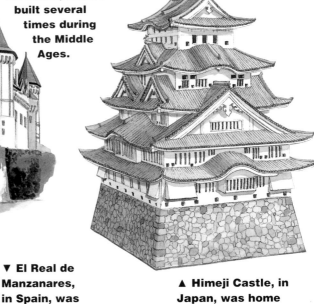

▲ Himeji Castle, in Japan, was home to Japanese knights called samurai.

Castles were built in many different styles. In France, castles usually had tall pointed roofs on their towers. Spanish castles often had highly decorated stonework or brickwork, which showed the influence of the Muslims called Moors. The main centre of castle building outside Europe was Japan. Here, castles had overhanging roofs and wooden keeps built on stone basements.

▼ El Real de Manzanares, in Spain, was built as a castle-palace in 1475.

▲ 1400s
Most European castles were no longer so heavily fortified. Herstmonceux in England had brick walls and large windows.

1400s Castle building declines in Europe.

1453 Constantinople falls to Turks, marking the end of the Middle Ages.

► 1800s
The fairytale-like castle of Neuschwanstein was built for Ludwig II, the mad king of Bavaria.

Knights and knaves

Alexander 'Nevsky'
(c. 1218–1263)
Russia's most famous knight, Alexander was the second son of the Grand Duke Yaroslav. In 1240 he defeated the Swedes on the banks of the River Neva and so won the name 'Nevsky'. In 1242 he defeated the Teutonic Order at Lake Peipus. However, he had to pay tribute to the Tartars who controlled much of Russia then.

Alexander 'Nevsky'

Bohemund of Taranto
(c. 1056–1111)
The son of Norman adventurer Robert Guiscard, Bohemund was Count of Apulia in southern Italy. He fought against the Byzantine empire in the 1080s and joined the First Crusade in 1096, with his cousin or nephew, Tancred. He ended up as Prince of Antioch, in Outremer, and spent three years as a prisoner of the Saracen leader Malik Ghazi before returning victoriously to Antioch.

Clare, Richard de ('Strongbow') (d. 1176)
Strongbow was the son of the first Earl of Pembroke, a part of south Wales seized by Norman invaders. In 1168 Dermot, King of Leinster, invited Strongbow to support him in his war with another Irish kingdom, Connaught. Strongbow crossed to Ireland in 1170, captured Dublin and Waterford and married Dermot's daughter. This invasion and marriage marked the start of Norman settlement in Ireland.

Colleoni, Bartolomeo
(1400–1475)
Born near Bergamo, in Italy, Colleoni was typical of his time. As a condottiere he fought for wages rather than out of loyalty to lord or state. During the wars between the Italian states of Milan and Venice, he fought for both sides – from 1454 he fought as a commander for Venice, where his statue still stands today.

Coucy, Enguerrand, seventh Sire de (1340–97)
Considered to be the most skilful French knight of his day, Enguerrand was Count of Soissons and Marle. Sent to England as a hostage, he married Isabella, daughter of King Edward III. He decided to remain neutral in the wars between England and France and went to fight in Italy, claiming land ruled by Austria. He was with the French forces defeated by the Turks at Nicopolis in Greece, and died shortly afterwards.

Edward the Black Prince
(1330–1376)
Edward was the eldest son of Edward III, king of England. He was later named after his black coat of arms, which included three silver ostrich plumes. The Black Prince fought at the Battle of Crécy in 1346 and went on to lead more daring raids into northern France, defeating the French at Poitiers. In 1362 he became Prince of Aquitaine and an ally of Pedro the Cruel, king of Castile and León in Spain.

El Cid

El Cid (c. 1034–1099)
Rodrigo, or Ruy, Díaz de Vivar is also known in Spain as Campeador, 'the Champion'. A knight in the service of King Alfonso VI, he was exiled and took service with the Moors. In 1093 he became a warlord in his own right and in 1094 captured Valencia, which he ruled until his death.

Guesclin, Bertrand du
(c. 1320–1380)
Born near Dinan in Brittany, du Guesclin was famously ugly. However he fought brilliantly against the English at Rennes, where he was made a knight, and at Dinan and Melun. He also battled with Charles the Bad of Navarre, at Cocherel. He became High Constable of France in 1370. Du Guesclin made the French knights more effective as an army, fighting on foot if necessary despite the traditions of chivalry. He paid his troops proper wages to stop them looting and killing the peasants, and he encouraged the use of gunpowder. He died during the siege of Châteauneuf-de-Rendon.

Guiscard, Robert (c. 1015–1085)
This knight took part in the Norman invasion of southern Italy and Sicily, when landless knights sought wealth and territory. He fought the Byzantine empire as well as the Saracens and championed the cause of the pope against the Roman Emperor, the German Henry IV.

Hawkwood, Sir John de
(c. 1320–1394)
Hawkwood was born the son of a tanner. Having fought at the battles of Crécy and Poitiers, he was knighted by King Edward III of England. In 1360 he became a mercenary, leading a famous company of English lances which fought for the cities of Pisa and Florence in the Italian wars.

John of Bohemia
(1296–1346)

The son of Count Henry III of Luxembourg, John fought for the Bavarians and in Italy and became King of Bohemia (now part of the Czech republic). Although he was blinded during a tournament, in 1346 he led 500 knights to Crécy, fighting for the French king Philip IV. Unable to see a thing, John had his knights tie the reins of his horse to theirs and advanced into the thick of the fighting, hacking and slashing with his sword. He was cut to pieces.

John of Gaunt (1340–1399)

The fourth son of King Edward III of England, John was born at Ghent ('Gaunt'). He became Duke of Lancaster in 1362. In 1372 he claimed the crown of Castile in Spain, through his second marriage, but he never gained the country. He did become Duke of Aquitaine and his descendants (through his third wife) became rulers of England.

le Meingre, Jean, 'Boucicaut'
(c. 1366–1421)

Becoming Marshal of France in 1391, Jean was captured by the Turks during an ill-fated Crusade in 1396, at Nicopolis in Greece. He was ransomed, became governor of Genoa in Italy, and was captured by the English at Agincourt in 1415. He died in Yorkshire, still a prisoner of war.

Jean le Meingre

Montfort, Simon de
(c. 1160–1218)

Of Norman descent, this Earl of Leicester led the cruel Crusade against the Cathars of southern France in 1208. He was killed during the siege of Toulon.

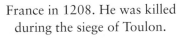

Simon de Montfort

Montfort, Simon de, (younger) (c 1208–1265)

Son of the above, this Earl of Leicester married the sister of Henry III of England and was sent to govern Gascony (today part of France). He soon fell out with the king and led the English barons (the powerful lords) in a civil war, setting up the first English parliament. He then quarrelled with the barons and was defeated at Evesham in 1265.

Owain Glyndwr (c. 1354–c. 1416)

This Welsh prince served as squire to the Earl of Arundel, but in 1400 fell into a feudal dispute with his English neighbour Reginald Grey, Lord of Ruthin. This triggered off a rising which turned into a full-scale Welsh war of independence. Owain gained support in Ireland, Scotland, France and in England too. The Welsh were defeated by the end of 1413, but Owain was never captured.

Percy, Sir Henry 'Hotspur'
(1364–1403)

The hot-headed son of the Earl of Northumberland, in England, Henry was already fighting at the age of 14. He battled against the French, the Scots and the Welsh, with whom he later allied himself. He was killed fighting against the king, Henry IV, at the Battle of Shrewsbury.

Richard I of England, 'Coeur de Lion' (1157–1199)

This king, the son of Henry II and Eleanor of Aquitaine, was a battling knight as much as a ruler, and won great admiration for his part in the Crusades. Acre surrendered to him, one of many victories. However, he failed to take Jerusalem and made peace with Saladin. Returning home, he was captured by Leopold, Duke of Austria, and handed over to his enemy, the Emperor Henry VI. A very high ransom had to be paid by the English people.

Tancred (1078–1112)

Tancred was of Norman descent, the son of Otho the Good. In 1096 he joined up with his relative Bohemund of Taranto on the First Crusade. He was a skilled soldier, taking part in sieges all over the Holy Land. He ended up as one of the most important rulers in Outremer, governing Tiberias, Antioch and Edessa.

Tancred

Wallace or Walays, Sir William (c. 1274–1305)

This Scottish knight began Scotland's war of independence against England, defeating Edward I at Stirling Bridge in 1297. Defeated in turn at Falkirk in 1298, he fled to France, but was captured back in Scotland in 1305. He was taken to London where he was hanged and beheaded. Then his body was cut in four and sent to the towns of Perth, Newcastle, Berwick and Stirling.

Wolfram von Eschenbach
(c. 1170–c. 1220)

Not all knights were famous for their battles. Wolfram was a minor knight who is best remembered as a poet, or Minnesänger. He was born near Anspach in Bavaria and joined the court of Hermann of Thuringia at Wartburg castle. He wrote one of the great tales of knighthood, *Parzival*.

Knights in fiction

Arthur

The historical Arthur was probably a British Celt of the sixth century AD. He may have been a general (dux) at the head of a long campaign against the Angles and Saxons who had invaded after the fall of the Roman empire. His name crops up in early Welsh myths and legends and by the later Middle Ages writers transformed him into a mighty king, the leader of the Knights of the Round Table. Tales of King Arthur's chivalry spread over Europe, and have inspired writers ever since.

Bedivere or Bedwyr

This figure appears in some of the earliest Welsh tales to mention King Arthur. In *Le Morte d'Arthur* by Sir Thomas Malory (*c.* 1469) he becomes one of the most important Knights of the Round Table. When Arthur lies dying, it is Bedivere who hurls his sword Excalibur into the lake.

Excalibur

The Canterbury knight

Geoffrey Chaucer (*c.* 1343–1400) was an English poet who wrote a series of tales as if they were being swapped by a group of pilgrims on the way to Canterbury. One of Chaucer's pilgrims is a knight, described as being chivalrous and brave. He is a veteran of 15 battles who has fought in wars against Turks and Moors, and yet is always gentle and polite. He has fought in tournaments and owns a fine set of horses. His tunic is stained with the marks of his armour.

Dietrich of Bern

Just as the warrior Arthur reappears in medieval tales as a splendid king, so does Theodoric reappear in German legends as Dietrich of Bern, a chivalrous knight. He features in the *Song of the Nibelungs*, a grim story of honour and revenge written down in Germany in the 1200s. The real Theodoric was a king of the Ostrogoths who died in 526.

Ector

According to *Le Morte d'Arthur*, the wizard Merlin placed the baby Arthur in the care of Sir Ector, to conceal from his enemies the fact that the boy was the son of Uther Pendragon. A recent version of the story appears in *The Once and Future King*, four Arthurian tales written by T H White in 1958. The first of these tales, *The Sword in the Stone*, was made into a film by Walt Disney.

Falstaff, Sir John

This humorous character was created by the English playwright William Shakespeare in the 1590s, although he may have been based on a real knight, Sir John Oldcastle. Falstaff is old, fat and jolly. He drinks and boasts a lot, but is really a coward. There were probably many knights like him in real life!

Galahad

The name Galahad appears in later stories about King Arthur. He is the son of Lancelot and the princess Elaine, and is the purest knight of all. He is the only knight to find the Holy Grail. The Grail was believed to be the cup from which Jesus drank at the Last Supper. According to legend it was brought to the British Isles. In fact the idea of the Grail probably began with ancient Celtic folktales about a magic cauldron.

Ganelon

Also known as Gan of Mayence or Gano of Moganza, he was one of Charlemagne's twelve special knights called paladins. Charlemagne (747–814) was king of the Franks and a battle in his campaign against the Moors in Spain gave rise to the heroic tale, the *Song of Roland*. In this tale the paladins are transformed into medieval knights. Ganelon betrays the ideals of chivalry and so brings about the death of Roland (another of the paladins).

Gareth ('Beaumains')

In the legends of King Arthur, Gareth is the son of Arthur's sister Morgawse and King Lot of Orkney. He arrives unknown at his uncle's court at Camelot, and is put to work in the kitchens. His fine hands are noticed by Kay, who calls him by the French name, Beaumains.

Gawain

The eldest brother of Gareth, Gawain is described as one of the bravest knights of Arthur's Round Table. In Welsh tales he was called Gwalchmai, in French, Gauvain. In one story he goes in search of a strange Green Knight. On the way his honour is tested in different ways.

Hagen

In the *Song of the Niebelungs*, written down in Germany in the 1200s, Hagen is a knight in service to the rulers of Burgundy.

He kills the hero Siegfried, whose widow later kills him and his comrades in turn.

Kay or Cai
This warrior also appears in ancient Welsh tales, where he is linked with Arthur and magical deeds. In later stories from England and France, he is shown as a boastful, hot-headed, clumsy knight, the foster-brother and steward of King Arthur.

Lancelot of the Lake
This Arthurian knight first appears in French versions of the tale. He is the son of King Ban of Benwick, in Brittany, and becomes the most handsome, honourable and daring Knight of the Round Table. He is the king's best friend, but falls in love with Arthur's wife, Guinevere. In the end, Lancelot becomes a monk, and Guinevere a nun.

Mordred, Modred or Medraut
In some tales Mordred is the son of Arthur, in others his nephew. It is the evil Mordred who brings the golden age of knighthood to an end. At the last great battle he is slain by Arthur, but wounds the king fatally in return.

Olivier
Also known as Oliver, Oliviero or Ulivieri, this knight appears in the French *Song of Roland* as a chivalrous and wise knight who becomes firm friends with Roland after they have fought each other.

Palamedes
This is the only non-Christian knight at the court of King Arthur, a noble Saracen.

Perceval of Galles
Known in the original Welsh tales as Peredur and in German romances as Parzival, Perceval's story dates back to ancient times. Later tales describe his search for the Holy Grail.

Don Quixote
This character was invented by the Spanish writer Miguel de Cervantes in the 1600s. He tells the story of a simple man who is so excited by the tales of chivalry he reads that he has himself knighted by an innkeeper, becoming 'Don Quixote'. This latterday knight lives in a fantasy world, jousting at windmills and fighting armies of sheep, accompanied by his servant Sancho Panza and his horse Rocinante.

Don Quixote

Robin of Locksley
According to some old English folk tales, the mythical outlaw and popular hero Robin Hood was actually a knight of the 12th century, born at Locksley in Nottinghamshire. He championed the poor people, robbing the rich to provide for them. Some stories say he was really Robert, Earl of Huntingdon.

Roland
The heroic knight described in the *Song of Roland* has his origins in history. He was one of the élite paladins of Charlemagne, and died in 778 fighting off a Basque ambush in a mountain pass at Roncesvalles in the Pyrenees. In Italian stories Roland is called Orlando.

Sheriff of Nottingham
In many folk tales the heroes are outlaws fighting against injustice.

One of the most famous of these tales is about the English hero Robin Hood. His great enemy is the Sheriff of Nottingham, the evil knight who governs the region around Sherwood Forest while King Richard I is away at the Crusades, though in medieval tales the king is Edward.

Siegfried
Siegfried (in Scandinavia, Sigurd) was a hero of ancient German myths. In the medieval *Song of the Nibelungs* he becomes a noble prince of the Rhineland who is murdered by Hagen.

St George
This Christian saint was originally a Roman soldier who died in AD 303. He was believed to have helped the Crusaders at Antioch and was later adopted as the patron saint of England, Aragon and Portugal. Since the Middle Ages he has always been shown as a chivalrous knight in armour, killing dragons and rescuing maidens.

St George

Tristan or Tristram
This hero is a knight serving King Mark of Cornwall. He is sent to Ireland to fetch Iseult (also known as Esyllt or Isolde), who is to be Mark's new bride. On the way back the couple accidentally drink a potion and fall hopelessly in love. The lovers flee to Brittany where Mark seeks out and fights Tristan, fatally wounding him. The story spread from Cornwall to Brittany, and from there to France and Germany.

Glossary

aketon A padded garment worn underneath mail armour, or as their only defence by some soldiers of lesser rank.

allegiance The loyalty owed by a vassal to his lord under the feudal system.

aketon

armourer A metal-worker who specialized in making armour.

banner A rectangular heraldic flag showing a coat-of-arms. Only one was made for each bearer of arms.

bard A set of armour designed for a warhorse.

battering ram A huge beam of wood with a metal tip used for knocking down gates.

battlements The defensive parapets on top of castle walls.

Black Death Various forms of the bubonic plague, a terrible illness which swept through Asia and Europe between the 1330s and 1350s. In places, it killed as many as one person in three.

castle A heavily fortified building, lived in by a whole community of people. Rich knights might have had many castles to defend their lands.

chivalry The ideals of knighthood, by which a knight is generous towards noble enemies and honourable towards women.

Christendom All the lands where people held the Christian faith.

coat-of-arms
The badge of a family or organization, drawn up according to the rules of heraldry. Originally named from the surcoat worn by the knight, the coat-of-arms appeared on shields and banners used in both battle and tournaments.

coat-of-arms

coif A hood made of mail and worn on the head. The helmet was worn on top of it, leaving the bottom edges of the coif to protect the neck.

condottiere An Italian knight who was contracted to fight for money. The contract, or condotta, was drawn up between the leader of the mercenary band and his employer and promised to provide a certain number of men for a particular conflict or battle.

constable A knight appointed by the king to hold a castle or look after royal interests.

courtly love The honouring of a woman by a knight, as idealized by the poets of southern France.

crossbow A very powerful bow. The first ones were stretched by hand, but the later versions used a variety of mechanisms. They shot arrows called bolts or quarrels.

Crusade A 'holy' war fought by Christians against people with different religious beliefs. These were mostly Moslems and sometimes heretical Christians.

curfew 1 An order to remain inside a town or at home at night. 2 A clay dome-shaped pot used to cover fires.

destrier A large warhorse of the best quality.

drawbridge A bridge which can be drawn up or let down to prevent entry to a castle.

dub To make someone a knight by placing the flat blade of a sword on their shoulders. In the early days of knighthood, knights were dubbed with a cuff of the hand.

crossbow

duchy A region ruled by a duke. Some duchies such as the Duchy of Burgundy were more powerful than small principalities and kingdoms.

falconry The training of birds of prey to hunt.

feudal system A social system common in the early Middle Ages, in which one person was granted land or protection by a lord in return for their services or labour.

garrison The troops stationed in a castle or fort.

gatehouse The complex of towers and gates which guards the entrance to a town or castle.

gauntlet A protective glove worn when fighting or hunting.

great hall The large hall in a castle, often used for dining.

guild An organization of skilled craftsmen or merchants.

hauberk A long tunic made of mail, used as armour.

herald An official working for a king or noble. He agreed the rules of battle with the enemy and carried messages between parties at war. He also knew all about heraldic devices, and after a battle listed the knights who had died.

heraldry The system of signs and family badges used on shields and flags from the Middle Ages onwards.

heretic Someone whose religious beliefs are thought to be sinful by religious leaders.

Holy Land The lands in the Middle East which are holy to Christians, Jews and Moslems.

jousting Combat during a tournament, in which one knight on horseback charges another with a lance.

keep A defensive stone tower at the centre of a castle, also known as a donjon.

knight A soldier who fought on horseback. During the European Middle Ages, knights were ranked among the nobility.

knight banneret A high-ranking knight who rode into battle under his own banner. He would often command several lances.

lance (1) A long spear, almost always carried on horseback. (2) A unit in a medieval army, led by a knight. This would be made up of the knight himself, mounted archers, often another mounted soldier, and a crossbowman and pikeman on foot.

longbow A long and powerful wooden bow which shot arrows. It was popular with archers in the British Isles.

lord A member of the most powerful group in society. Nobles and the king himself were part of this group.

mace A heavy club, normally used by a knight to attack the enemy.

mail A fabric made of interlinking iron rings, used as armour.

mangonel A kind of giant catapult, used to knock down castle walls.

mêlée A general fight, staged as a competition in a tournament.

mercenary A soldier who hires out his services for money.

mews Sheds used for falconry. A mew was the cage in which hawks were kept while moulting (shedding feathers).

Middle Ages A term used by historians to describe the period between the end of the Roman empire in AD 476 and the start of our modern world in about 1500.

moat A water-filled ditch around a castle which made it harder for enemies to attack.

Moor One of the peoples of north Africa, especially a Berber or Arab. For over 500 years the Moors also lived in Spain.

mail

mortar 1 A mixture used to bind stones or bricks together. 2 A bowl used for grinding herbs and spices.

motte A steep earth mound which supported the towers of early castles.

nef A boat-shaped dish which held napkins and table knives.

order A religious organization of monks or knights.

page A young boy who served a noble family as part of his training for knighthood.

peasant A country dweller who worked on the land.

pennon A small flag carried on a cavalry lance, including a badge, coat-of-arms or colours. Pennons were flown by a lord's retainers.

pestle A stick or rod for grinding up herbs and spices.

pilgrim A person who travels to a holy shrine or city. Christians went mainly to Jerusalem and Rome, Moslems to Mecca.

plate armour Armour made out of sheets of solid metal. This was also known as white armour.

pope The leader of the Roman Catholic Church.

portcullis A heavy grille used to seal off a castle gateway.

principality A region ruled by a prince.

quintain A target on a post, used for practice with a lance.

ransom The fee paid for the release of a captured knight.

quintain

retainer One of a knight's armed followers. The knight supplied his retainers' horses and weapons.

samurai The Japanese land-owning and fighting class that was the nearest equivalent to the knights of medieval Europe.

Saracen The European word for a Moslem warrior, normally an Arab, Turk or Kurd.

scabbard The sheath or casing for the blade of a sword.

scullion A very junior servant who worked in the kitchen.

sentry The guard at a gate or bridge.

serf Someone who had to work on the land under the feudal system.

siege The cutting off or blockade of a town or castle, in order to starve it, attack it and make it surrender.

solar The private living room, usually off the great hall, in a medieval castle or manor house.

spur A point or wheel fitted to the heel of a rider, used to make a horse go faster.

squire A youth who was in training for knighthood. He served a knight for several years.

standard A flag flown to mark the rallying point on a battlefield or the headquarters of the bearer of arms. It was normally swallow-tailed.

stirrup A support for the foot when riding on horseback.

sumpter A horse or mule used to carry baggage.

tilt (1) A barrier erected between two jousting knights. (2) To joust.

tournament A mock battle, for amusement or training.

trapper A horse covering made of cloth or mail, used both in battle and in peacetime.

trebuchet A siege machine used for hurling rocks against a castle's walls. Sometimes dead animals were also thrown over the walls to spread disease.

trencher Originally a slice of stale bread used as a plate or dish-liner. Later the word was used to mean a plate made of wood or metal.

undermine To tunnel underneath a wall so that it collapsed.

vassal Anyone who was granted land by a feudal lord in return for services.

vigil Staying awake, being on watch, or praying all night before being made a knight.

wardrobe A small room, usually next to the lord's bedroom, for storing clothes and working out household accounts.

wattle and daub A mixture of wood, clay, straw and animal hair used to construct timber buildings.

vigil

Index

Acknowledgements

Consultants: **Brian Davison, Christopher Gravett**
Indexer: **Sue Lightfoot**

The publishers would like to thank the following
illustrators for their contributions to this book:

Julian Baker 5cr, 12cl, 21r, 29tl, 31r, 34bl, 36tr/c, 49b, 51tl, 52cl, 54br, 55tl,
56br, 57b, 73tr, 84–85; **Gino D'Achille** (Artists' Partners) 56–57t, 60–61,
74–75; **Peter Dennis** (Linda Rogers Associates) 18–19, 27, 32–33, 36–39, 46r,
54tl, 55br, 59br, 64–67, 68–69c, 74tl, 75br, 77tr; **Francesca D'Ottavi** 16–17;
Les Edwards (Arena) 14l, 15tr, 15br, 78–79; **Terry Gabbey** (Associated
Freelance Artists Ltd) 22–23, 30–31; **Martin Hargreaves** (Illustration) 52–53;
Stephen Holmes 43tl; **Adam Hook** (Linden Artists) 44b, 46cl, 68cl; **Christa
Hook** (Linden Artists) 44t, 45br; **Christian Hook** 81; **Tudor Humphries** 41r,
47tr, 49tr; **John James** (Temple Rogers Artists' Agents) 24–25, 40; **Eddy
Krähenbühl** 20–21, 28–29, 48b; **Angus McBride** (Linden Artists) 4–5, 12–13,
62–63, 76–77; **Danuta Mayer** 10–11, 50–51; **Clare Melinsky** 86–91;
Nicki Palin 6–7, 32tr, 34–35l/c, 41tl, 42r, 43r, 58–59, 80; **Mark Peppé**
(B.L.Kearley Ltd) 7t, 51tr, 56bl, 61r, 72tr; **Richard Phipps** (Illustration) 8–9;
Clive Spong (Linden Artists) 15tl, 60bl, 70tl, 72bl, 75cr, 76t, 78bl;
Shirley Tourret (B.L.Kearley Ltd) 21t, 22l, 23r, 26c/b, 29tr/br, 35bl/tr/c,
36bl, 37tr, 38t, 39br, 41tr, 42l, 43tr, 45tr, 47b, 66l, 68l, 69r;
Bob Venables (Thorogood Illustration) 70–71.

Chapter illuminations by **Danuta Mayer**
Woodcuts by **Anthony Colbert** (B.L.Kearley Ltd)

The publishers would also like to thank the following for
supplying photographs for this book:

AKG London: 5tr; **Bibliothèque Nationale, Paris:** 82tl;
Board of Trustees of the Royal Armouries: 82b; **Bridgeman Art Library:** 11br,
14br, 48tr, 62tr; **British Library:** 26tr, 65cr, 69tr; **Corbis UK Ltd:** 33br, 71br,
74br; **E.T. Archive:** 6tr, 8tr, 13tr, 76bc; **Mary Evans Picture Library:** 19tr;
Fotomas Index: 83tl; **Fine Art Photographs:** 82cr; **Ronald Grant Archive:**
83tr/cl/cr/br; **Hampshire County Council:** 82cl; **Peter Newark's Pictures:** 17cl,
78cl; **Popperfoto:** 81br; **Royal Geographical Society:** 84-85tc; **Scala:** 52bl;
Society of Antiquaries of London: 25tr.